# THE INSTINCTUAL TRAUMA RESPONSE & DUAL-BRAIN DYNAMICS

## A GUIDE FOR TRAUMA THERAPY

Louis Tinnin, M.D., & Linda Gantt, Ph.D., ATR-BC
### The ITR Training Institute
Morgantown, West Virginia

833-847-8437
www.helpfortrauma.com

**ISBN 978-0-9850162-2-7**

Gargoyle Press
364 Patteson Drive, Suite #105
Morgantown, WV 26505
Email: gargoylepress.us@gmail.com

Cover Design by *Rachael Marr*
Shutterstock photo

*Available thorough Create Space, Amazon Books*

## *Endorsements*

This is a ground-breaking book of great insight and clarity. Drs. Tinnin and Gantt have constructed a theoretical model for the neurophysiology of trauma that shatters the barriers of the DSM-IV, and offers fresh insights in the structure of trauma, with powerful implications for its treatment. They have made the best case yet for the role of dissociation in the clinical manifestations of trauma, introducing the split-brain concept of the suppression of left brain consciousness by the non-verbal, somatically-oriented right brain in the production of the dissociative state, linking it inexorably to the all-important dorsal vagal freeze response.

The therapeutic implications of this concept are profound, and are addressed in detail, providing theory and application of techniques that embrace both cognitive and non-verbal somatic/behavioral elements. This is a comprehensive, highly intelligent book that provides new hope for the difficult-to-treat dissociative, complex trauma patient."

*Robert Scaer, MD*

*Author of The Body Bears the Burden, The Trauma Spectrum and Eight Keys to Body-Brain Balance.*

At last! Colleagues and students from all over the world have waited for Drs. Tinnin and Gantt to publish the definitive account of their innovative and highly effective trauma therapy. With its strong roots in neurobiological theory and its chapters on application to each of the primarily trauma based disorders, this volume is worth the wait. It is at once a practical therapy guide and a trauma theory reference that clinicians of all persuasions and experience levels will treasure. Only rarely does a work not only increase our knowledge, but lend us a new way of understanding a phenomenon. *The Instinctual Trauma Response and Dual Brain Dynamics* is such a book.

*Hugh Marr, PhD*

Private Practice, Alexandria, VA
Adjunct Faculty in Trauma Therapy, Argosy University
Co-author, *What Story Are You Living?*

Drs. Tinnin and Gantt are extraordinary pioneers in the field of trauma treatment, and this long-awaited book is a shining jewel! Their skillful blending of hypnosis, video technology, and art within the context and structure of the Instinctual Trauma Response model allows for the gentle and rapid processing of haunting traumatic memories in a matter of days, not months or years. Their sensitivity and compassion, along with their exceptionally astute understanding of trauma and the healing process, have produced a significant breakthrough in the field of trauma treatment. I applaud their work, and enthusiastically recommend this book to all those who treat and support survivors of trauma

*Glenn Schiraldi, Ph.D., LTC (USAR, Ret.)*

University of Maryland School of Public Health
Founder, Resilience Training International
([www.resiliencefirst.com](www.resiliencefirst.com)).
Author of *The Post-Traumatic Stress Disorder Sourcebook, The Complete Guide to Resilience, The Self-Esteem Workbook.*

It is a tremendous pleasure to be able to recommend this book to all who treat those who have had traumatic experiences resulting in psychological suffering. Whether acute or sustained, the effects of trauma on the brain can lead not only to anguish for the patient, but also to frustration for the clinician. These painful conditions, so often resistant to even the most sophisticated therapies, are now, thanks to the dedication of Drs. Tinnin and Gantt, able to be approached with a new and remarkably successful methodology. I have admired these two explorers for decades; they remind me of Freud in their search for the most felicitous theory to explain and then to treat the effects of trauma. Their focus on the evidence in their clinical work, and their creativity in developing new and ever more widely applicable techniques, is a model for responsible and effective care. I hope that all therapists will read, re-read, and learn from this excellent book.

*Judith A. Rubin, Ph.D., ATR-BC*

Department of Psychiatry, University of Pittsburgh
Emeritus Faculty, Pittsburgh Psychoanalytic Institute
Author, *Artful Therapy, Introduction to Art Therapy, The Art of Art Therapy*; Editor, *Approaches to Art Therapy*
Past President and Honorary Life Member, American Art Therapy Association

## *Acknowledgements*

The brief intensive trauma therapy program (Intensive Trauma Therapy, Inc.) that we developed in Morgantown, West Virginia, made it possible to test and refine the clinical methods we describe here. The most important contributors were five of our therapists. Ann DiMarco, social worker and play therapist, showed that our methods could be adapted to the treatment of children as young as three. Carrie Downey, social worker, developed the thorough intake process to support our maxim, "Treat Trauma First." Carrie Swart and Kristin Johnson-Gibeaut, counselors, were our guides and models for the careful development of parts work. The most recent addition to the team was another counselor, Jonathan Pishner, who had used our procedures in community settings. We thank them for their dedication and good work.

# *Preface*

This book is controversial for two reasons. The first is that some therapists and researchers have difficulty accepting the dual brain model's two minds—the verbal and nonverbal. The second is our insistence that, when treating post-traumatic disorders, it is better to process the traumas first. Both controversies have been fueled by what we hold to be enduring misconceptions. One is the attitude that right brain/left brain notions are simplistic and cannot account for the complexity of the one brain. The other is the insistence on a lengthy phase-oriented treatment; beginning with what is often years of supportive stabilization, followed by emotionally expressive trauma processing, finishing with a final phase of consolidation. In the past, we subscribed to this model. However, we now consider a prolonged period of stabilization (especially one spanning years) unnecessary. As we show in our discussion of dissociative regression, we can proceed with trauma work once the regression has been reversed and we give specific information about how to do so.

When we assumed that trauma therapy necessarily required reliving the traumatic experience and releasing the vehement emotion, we thought that abreaction was necessary. We persevered even though an abreaction sometimes overwhelmed our attempts at slowing it down or required a fractionating of the emotional catharsis. We worried that the explosive abreactions were traumatic on their own for both patient and therapist. We saw that the course of trauma therapy was complicated by the patient's fearful aversion to talking about the specifics of the traumatic experience, which seemed to get worse each time we approached the story. Eventually, we came to see that this trauma phobia deprived many of the treatment they needed.

Our clinical approach changed when we realized that abreaction was not necessary. We saw how trauma phobia can be adequately handled by the experience of a successful trauma processing. We learned that a necessary goal of trauma processing is to gain narrative closure to the nonverbal traumatic memory, which renders it past tense and immune to current triggers. We developed standard procedures for objective study of the traumatic event and for casting the verbal and nonverbal experiences into a narrative structure for long-term memory storage.

This did require some modifications to treatment-as-usual. Sessions longer than the 50-minute hour are necessary for the initial narrative processing. Usually this amounts to scheduling 90 minutes for the session. However, the subsequent graphic narrative processing can be divided and scheduled for 50-minute sessions as needed.

Our approach makes it possible to tell the story without reliving it, shortens the time needed to complete trauma therapy, and teaches empowering techniques that outlast the therapy sessions. Successful trauma processing prepares one to continue the work without fear and, finally, to use our standard procedures on one's own in self-help after-care. We hope our readers will see the logic and utility of our approach and will be inspired to try our methods.

# TABLE OF CONTENTS

# INTRODUCTION

## *Today's Intensive Trauma Therapy Program*

Intensive Trauma Therapy, Inc. (ITT) is a freestanding outpatient clinic in Morgantown, West Virginia, devoted to treatment, research, and training in the field of trauma-related problems. The treatment program for post-traumatic conditions [primarily post-traumatic stress disorder (PTSD) and the dissociative disorders] consists of a series of therapeutic procedures designed to accomplish specific tasks. A multidisciplinary team delivers the procedures, with each member trained to conduct every procedure. The patients relate to ITT as their provider rather than to a single therapist. This approach is quite different from contemporary outpatient mental health programs but it is very much like its first incarnation as an inpatient treatment program we developed for psychosis in the 1970s (Tinnin, 1977).

The techniques and procedures we use today derive from the theory we developed and modified as we worked in different settings. There were three distinct phases in this development:

### 1970s: Ego boundary diffusion model

In the mid-1970s, we worked in the psychiatric unit of Prince George's General Hospital in Cheverly, Maryland, just over the border from Washington, DC. Lou was the chief of psychiatry, and Linda was the art therapist. The treatment milieu we had carefully cultured on our open-door unit was caving in to the increasing proportion of regressed patients who could not benefit from conventional talking treatment. It was evident that these patients had lost their capacity for verbal communication and self-regulation. They could not maintain reality testing and, when surrounded by other patients, they showed a rapidly decreasing ability to differentiate the boundaries between themselves and others. They even lost the boundary between inside and outside their own bodies. They needed something besides talking to help them restore those boundaries and recover their sense of reality.

Our answer was to develop a sub-unit for the acutely psychotic and severely depressed patients, organized around nonverbal therapies. The program consisted of art therapy and movement therapy

1

procedures designed to repair ego boundary diffusion. We were careful to maintain an optimal level of stimulation. We devised procedures to restore a sense of time and duration and to promote the ability to act with intention and direction. We provided hands-on assistance and encouragement in simple activities leading toward mastery. We christened this program "The Prince George's Model" (Tinnin, 1977) and wrote about the innovative nonverbal procedures (Gantt, 1979a). Today's ITT outpatient program applies updated versions of these procedures to the treatment of chronic mental illness.

There is a similar re-birth of our early treatment procedures in our present-day program for children and adolescents. We did our first graphic trauma narrative with a child hospitalized in Prince George's Hospital in 1974 (Gantt, 1979b). He was a nine-year-old burn victim on the pediatric ward with flashbacks of the explosive gasoline fire that burned his legs. After a flashback, he dialed the hospital switchboard and screamed, "Fire!" The telephone operator alerted the pediatric staff; they requested a psychiatric consultation the next day. The boy drew a picture story of his entire traumatic experience with a clear beginning, middle, and end. That was all that was needed. He had no more flashbacks, and his worried demeanor gave way to smiles. This was our first glimmer of the power of narrative trauma processing. The Prince George's Model defined six basic psychological functions that were critical to an individual's self-boundary. Our terms for these functions were identity (self as unitary agent), volition (capacity to act with intention and direction), time (sense of duration and sequence, as well as a connection between past and future), perception (differentiation of self and environment), body image (self as object) and symbolization (verbal). We came to understand these functions as representing a core group of autonomous ego functions as defined by Hartman (1958). Ego boundary diffusion meant that one or more of these functions was weakened. That deficiency became the target of our nonverbal therapies.
We were influenced by the writing of Sidney Blatt and Cynthia Wild through their book, *Schizophrenia: A Developmental Analysis* (1976). They systematically examined the hypothesis that schizophrenia involves developmental disturbances in the capacity to establish and maintain boundaries. They believed that boundary formation was basic to ego function. That capacity arose during

infant development through sequences of frustration and gratification that led to differentiation between self and non-self as well as a sense of continuity and permanence of objects. We thought our ego boundary model was a step forward. But we were soon to learn that we needed to question the assumption of mental unity that was a given in our psychoanalytic background.

## 1980s: Cerebral dominance theory

Early in the 1980s, we had the opportunity to examine a patient whose uncontrolled seizures had been relieved by a surgical severing of his corpus callosum, the bridge of nerve axons carrying information between his cerebral hemispheres. He had no direct communication between his right and left brains. He was in a day hospital due to his extraordinary "Dr. Strangelove" syndrome in which the left half of his body would take offense and attack the right half. The art therapist working with him encouraged him to allow his left hand to draw and to acknowledge the different opinions of his left side. He decided on a name for his left side and became able to speak aloud to inform the left side of his intentions and plans. He improved, and his left leg stopped trying to thrust him into the path of vehicles in the street or throw him out of the shower.

We read the report of Gazzaniga and Volpe on their split-brain studies and the implications for psychiatry (Gazzaniga & Volpe, 1981). These split-brain operations exposed the existence of two minds in an individual. The verbal mind was dominant; the nonverbal mind was silent and usually submissive but often harbored opinions and personality traits of its own. We puzzled about what this might mean for our conception of ego boundaries. Might there be two egos? Would there be dual ego boundaries and corresponding autonomous ego functions?

We finally read Julian Jaynes (1976) and began to understand the verbal and nonverbal brains. We concluded that the autonomous ego functions were language constructs in which verbal thinking invokes unitary subjects and objects and linear causality. The ego, then, is language-based and has a location in the language areas of the left hemisphere. To quote from Lou's seminal paper:

> *There is a curious behavior observed in the human split-brain experiments in which the subject demonstrates a*

3

*reflexive and obligatory ownership of the actions initiated by the silent right brain even though the speaking self is ignorant of that volition. If you add to this observation the results of another experiment, revealing the existence of a boundary to the verbal mental system in the intact brain, then—with the knowledge of certain facts about cerebral laterality—you may come to a startling conclusion: There exists a governing mental system that occupies the verbally dominant hemisphere and is responsible for mental unity, volition, and consciousness. I contend that this anatomical brain agency is the substrate for the ego. If this is true, then it can be seen that the ego, in its development, function, and integrity, is intimately involved in the brain dynamics of obligatory unity, cerebral dominance, and laterality (Tinnin, 1989, p. 404).*

We began to speculate that if there were one latent mental system in the nonverbal right hemisphere there might be more. Could it be possible under certain conditions to have multiple latent egos, each with its own traits, opinions, and agendas?

We had treated several outpatients over the years with the diagnosis of multiple personality disorder (now termed "dissociative identity disorder"). We did what we could with a psychodynamic approach but we knew that we really did not understand the disorder. We suspected that a good explanation of multiple personality disorder would open the way to a broader theory of how the mind works. By 1990, we had attended many workshops and a variety of national conferences on dissociative disorders. We learned valuable clinical lore about therapeutic relationships and emotionally evocative psychotherapy but little about how the brain can contain multiple selves.

## 1990s: Instinctual Trauma Response theory

During the time we were studying psychosis we saw many cases of brief reactive psychoses with sudden onset, extreme agitation, and quick recovery after just days or weeks. Upon recovery, these individuals would often be apparently normal, only to break down again later into a raving psychosis. While we were on the medical school faculty of West Virginia University we read Bessel Van der Kolk's book *Psychological Trauma* (1987). It contains a chapter

4

that describes the case of a woman who survived the Coconut Grove nightclub fire disaster of 1942. For years—on the anniversary of the trauma— she reenacted her escape from the flames. Each year the doctors would admit her to the hospital and treat her condition as an excited schizophrenic psychosis. The book chapter described how someone finally heard the patient's story and understood her condition as a form of post-traumatic flashback. When Dr. John King, the attending psychiatrist on the psychiatric intensive care unit at West Virginia University, read about the Coconut Grove patient he suspected that a substantial number of the patients admitted to his unit in an acute psychosis might also be post-traumatic. Lou was experienced in conducting amytal interviews, so Dr. King began consulting him for amytal interviews on patients admitted with sudden-onset psychotic states. After conducting seventy amytal interviews with Dr. King's patients, Lou determined that the psychosis in approximately half of the cases was related to trauma.

This experience was pivotal for our emerging interest in trauma. It was not just that many patients admitted with the diagnosis of bipolar disorder or schizophrenia were actually suffering post-traumatic syndromes. We discovered that the catharsis of reliving the traumatic experience was not the curative element for those patients that benefited from the amytal procedure. Lou videotaped the interviews and reviewed them with the patient within the next day or so. Many patients could not remember the contents of the session. At first, we were disappointed by those interviews in which the patient recited the traumatic experience in a matter-of-fact manner. We had predicted that those patients who did not get emotional would not benefit from the procedure. It turned out just the opposite. Those whose narratives were unemotional but complete—that is, not interrupted because of painful reliving—did better than those whose stories were emotionally told but interrupted before the ending. In the videotape reviews we could see that those who succeeded in telling the whole story and bringing it to an ending past the point of danger gained the relief that came with closure. Even those individuals that were painfully emotional got relief if they managed to finish the story and could assimilate the story when they reviewed the tape.

Thus began our interest in narrative trauma processing. We had yet to learn that narrative closure was not enough to fully recover from trauma and we were yet to learn that access to nonverbal (dissociated) memory was critical.

We saw that most people could not simply describe their traumatic experience without gaps in the story. Most people could remember their startle and flight reaction, but few would spontaneously remember being frozen in place or having an altered state of consciousness. It was necessary to get past the defenses of the verbal mind in order to gain an unbroken narrative. Lou then compared several methods for getting to the traumatic material. The amytal interview worked well. So did hypnosis. So did the so-called "laughing gas," nitrous oxide. It seemed that anything that sedated the left brain might get around the verbal defenses. However, we found that methods of nonverbal expression worked even when the verbal brain was not sedated. Without the complications of anesthesia or hypnosis, people could draw the whole story of their trauma with a little firm direction by the therapist.

Art therapy became our preferred approach to trauma processing. The thousands of graphic narratives that our patients constructed provided a major revelation about trauma. We saw that the human response to being trapped in a traumatic event was the same as the response of an animal prey captured by a predator. If fight or flight is blocked, the individual animal or person freezes. In humans, the universal freeze state tends to produce an altered state of consciousness.

We learned that the freeze and the altered state of consciousness in humans represented the mental state associated with relinquishing of dominance by the verbal brain. We soon found that the relinquishing of cerebral dominance in the trauma response resulted in psychological dissociation from consciousness of the traumatized self and that full healing requires a repair of that dissociation. Narrative trauma processing is necessary for recovery but it is not sufficient. The frozen traumatized self must be rescued and reunited with the survivor. We will later describe the externalized dialogue procedure we developed for repair of traumatic dissociation.

Knowing that dissociated selves result from trauma made it possible to understand the multiple dissociated selves that plague some victims of multiple traumas. Now we could apply the knowledge of ego boundary diffusion and cerebral dominance to treat patients with multiple personalities.

꙾   ꙾   ꙾

# *The Organization of This Book*

This book is divided into four parts. Part 1 introduces the concept of the normal duality of mind concealed by an obligatory illusion of unity. The concealed second mind is the nonverbal mind. Our examination of nonverbal thought and nonverbal memory reveals a startling system of brain dynamics involving cerebral dominance and its role in the Instinctual Trauma Response and dissociation. Part 1 finishes with descriptions of post-traumatic symptoms and the range of complications of trauma.

Part 2 describes methods of assessment and treatment based on the Instinctual Trauma Response model. Conventional treatment approaches spend considerable time and care in the first phase of treatment to promote stabilization of the patient before commencing trauma processing. We understand that the greatest risk of trauma therapy lies in the patient's dissociative regression. The supportive measures to reverse dissociative regression are uncomplicated and usually brief. Our approach to trauma therapy eschews abreaction or emotional reliving of the traumatic experiences. We aim to bring closure to the trauma narratives and to repair traumatic dissociation. The way we use art therapy and video therapy empowers patients to take charge of and complete their therapeutic tasks without hesitation.

Part 3 focuses on the treatment of specific syndromes such as post-traumatic stress disorder, dissociative disorders, somatic dissociation, medical and surgical trauma, and the special problems of survivors of orphanages.

Part 4 describes an innovative marathon treatment program and the adaptation of these treatment methods in traditional outpatient treatment by a solo therapist. This part also describes group therapy programs and the application of dual-brain methods to children and adolescents.

At the end of the book, we contemplate the future of the Instinctual Trauma Response model.

*Names of the individuals in the case examples are pseudonyms.*

# PART 1: DUAL-BRAIN THEORY

Humans are double-minded. They have dual brains and dual minds. Yet, they do not know it. They have not known it since they first became toddlers using speech and verbal memory. That happens around age three when the two cerebral hemispheres begin to exchange information across their maturing connection, the corpus callosum. When one hemisphere becomes dominant over the other, a compelling illusion of unity develops. This is when the individual acquires "I-ness" and begins life as a unitary agent in the world of verbal communication. The dominant hemisphere (usually the left) becomes the verbal brain, with a mind that operates by the logic of language and imposes a sense of self as unitary agent with willed action in linear time (past, present, future).

Dominant verbal consciousness rarely yields to the nonverbal mind except during one's instinctual response to trauma when cerebral dominance surrenders to nonverbal survival instincts. When the person recovers from the lapse of unity caused by trauma, the instinctual experience remains outside of verbal recall, unremembered in words but unforgettable in feelings and images. The nonverbal mind, unconstrained by narrative structure, remembers it all: the fear, the thwarted impulse to escape, the near-death experience of the freeze, the altered state of consciousness, the automatic obedience, and finally self-repair (as in animal wound-licking).

We contend that it is nonverbal memory of the traumatic survival experience, held as unfinished and forever present but outside of verbal consciousness, that causes post-traumatic intrusive, avoidant, arousal, and dissociative symptoms. Understanding the brain dynamics of cerebral dominance, verbal and nonverbal thought and memory, and the interaction of verbal and nonverbal minds can lead to specific therapeutic measures for such disorders.

## *Development of the Dual Brain*

Within the skull, the major portion of the human brain is divided at the midline into right and left hemispheres. A bridge of tissue—the corpus callosum—connects the half-brains and carries their exchange of information. The dual brain theory holds that each hemisphere has a mind of its own with a different form of thought and memory (Zaidel, 1994). Usually the left brain, with its language and computational capacity, is the dominant hemisphere, while the right brain is specialized for nonverbal thought and for the silent management of the autonomic nervous system (Bogen, 1990; Sperry, 1985). When the brain is surgically divided by midline sectioning of the corpus callosum, the left brain is able to speak its mind while the right brain is unable to express itself either in speech or in writing.

At birth, the nerve fibers of the corpus callosum have not completed their maturation. The nerve axons have yet to develop their insulating sheaths, and the naked fibers are unable to transmit information between the hemispheres. The maturation of the corpus callosum around age three (Salamy 1978) marks the completion of the brain's infrastructure for personhood. This prepares for the psychological birth of the individual (Mahler, Pine, & Bergman, 1975). This is the point when the verbal cerebral hemisphere takes charge by assuming the identity of this person and relegating the nonverbal hemisphere to the "it" of the brain (Tinnin, 1989). It is the left hemisphere that becomes dominant in the vast majority of people.

Before age three, the child has two minds operating in tandem with relatively little communication between them. It is only when the corpus callosum opens up neural transmission between the right and left hemispheres that the question of permanent dominance can be settled. Two phenomena happen then. The verbal brain claims selfhood, and the nonverbal hemisphere selflessly takes on the job of managing the body's nonintellectual functions. The right brain becomes a dedicated follower to the leading left brain.

## Cerebral dominance

The evolutionary achievement of mental unity through the governance of the dominant verbal hemisphere enabled humans to better master the environment through willful communication and self-conscious decision and planning (Tinnin, 1990). However, self-governance was attained at a dear price. Not only were humans doomed to self-deceit in service of the illusion of mental unity but also to the compromise of some of the brain's highest capacities. What had been compromised can be seen liberated in cases of "savant syndrome" in which virtuoso levels of nonverbal

10

performance escape the tyranny of a weakened left hemisphere. The agent of mental unity in the verbal hemisphere is the "I" of the mind. The obligatory assertion of mental unity obscures the fact that one's subjective consciousness is only a small part of one's mental life.

Consciousness is thus constricted by the obligatory maintenance of mental unity. There are also other constraints on consciousness that are powerful in their own right. These have to do with the fundamental opposition between the verbal conscious mind and the nonverbal mind. Consciousness maintains a mental representation of self and objects, which is laid out in a linear, sequential manner along the axis of time (Jaynes, 1976). Therefore, conscious thinking is verbally symbolized, linear, and sequential. These are all elements of Aristotelian logic (so called because Aristotle was the first to formulate the laws of conscious logic). These elements are intrinsically incompatible with the organization of the nonconscious mind.

## Verbal and nonverbal minds

The conscious mind employs a method of thought that is adaptive to historical recording, planning for the future, and interacting with other minds. The structure of verbal thought depends on a relatively few language constructs: identity, will, objective time, reality monitoring, body image, and symbolization. These are known as "the autonomous ego functions" (Tinnin, 1989; Hartman, 1958). When cerebral dominance is weakened or lost, it is this set of functions that fail.

Outside of consciousness is a vast domain of silent mental activity with its own nonverbal output that bypasses verbal censorship and gains expression as emotion, autonomic arousal (blood pressure, pulse, etc.), covert motor behavior (posture, gesture, etc.), inspiration, intuition, and other nonverbal cognitive or artistic expressions. However, when these expressions of the silent mind are detected by consciousness, they are either reflexively claimed and owned by rationalization or confabulation or are disowned by denial or neglect. Consciousness refuses to acknowledge "alien" initiative, remaining always loyal to its first priority, the maintenance of mental unity.

11

The nonverbal mind is not organized by the autonomous ego functions. Nonverbal thought is free of the law of unity and is not limited by unitary identity, clock time or sequence, or concerns about will, body image, or speech. The nonverbal mind is most comfortable with fluid identity, equivalence of past and present, and "scrapbook" storage of memory fragments. Its symbolization is not ruled by linguistics, and words are not the necessary elements of thought. Thinking may be simultaneous rather than sequential. This is the ungrammatical realm of nonverbal logic. The nonverbal mind depends entirely on input from the verbal brain for narrative context (Gazzaniga, 2000). Memories stored in the nonverbal mind without narrative organization could be experienced as in the present as well as past when they are activated.

These attributes of the unconscious nonverbal mind can be seen in the language of dreams, myths, and fantasy and in extraordinary first-person accounts by victims of left-brain strokes. Jill Bolte Taylor is a brain scientist who suffered a massive stroke in her left hemisphere and wrote a book about her experience, *My Stroke of Insight* (Taylor, 2006). She wrote:

> *Prior to this experience with stroke, the cells in my left hemisphere had been capable of dominating the cells in my right hemisphere. The judging and analytical character in my left mind dominated my personality. When I experienced the hemorrhage, and lost my left hemisphere language center cells that defined my self, those cells could no longer inhibit the cells in my right mind. As a result, I have gained a clear delineation of the two very distinct characters cohabitating my cranium. The two halves of my brain don't just perceive and think in different ways at a neurological level, but they demonstrate very different values based upon the types of information they perceive, and thus exhibit very different personalities. My stroke of insight is that at the core of my right hemisphere consciousness is a character that is directly connected to my feeling of deep inner peace. It is completely committed to the expression of peace, love, joy, and compassion in the world (p. 133).*

The different nature of thought in the verbal and nonverbal minds has been thoroughly discussed by others, especially Arieti (1976) writing about secondary and primary process thought. Even though present in each person's mind, the form of the nonconscious realm is difficult to imagine. It may be as difficult to grasp the concept of simultaneous thought, for example, as it is to visualize Einstein's concept of the universe. However, some insights have been suggested. An extraordinary image of one among many transient unconscious mental landscapes was offered by Oliver Sacks (1987) in his discussion of the remarkable capacity of autistic savant twins to generate prime numbers. He thought that they could mentally summon up and wander freely in great landscapes of numbers spatialized in a system of geometric harmonics. The ordinary person, however, is estranged from such nonconscious worlds by constructed symbols of reality laid out on the mind-space of mental representation.

The savant syndrome is a condition in which persons who are severely developmentally delayed or autistic, possess an exceptional capacity or skill. Such skills may be shown in music, memory, art, calculation, or certain other nonverbal areas. The verbal functioning of these individuals is handicapped due to brain damage from pre-natal, peri-natal, or post-natal injury (Treffert, 2009). The savant syndrome is usually manifested around the time of language acquisition and results in an impaired capacity for verbal symbolization (Victor, 1983). It is more common in the autistic population, occurring in one out of ten, whereas it is found in only one out of 2000 institutionalized developmentally delayed persons (Rimland & Fein, 1988).

The condition is usually permanent with the special skills remaining constant, whereas the skills are sometimes lost in the autistic savant as verbal and social skills increase. There are two basic capacities imbedded in many of the special talents. These are an ability for lightening processing of large amounts of data and a special memory facility, permitting instantaneous display of eidetic imagery of vast durations of time. Commonly, the individual can remember via photographic visual images of day-to-day events from years past and can quote time and place of minute trivial incidents. The calendar calculators can instantly name what day of the week a date falls over a range of thousands of years into the past or future.

## Dominance and inhibition

Cerebral dominance of the left hemisphere for verbal symbolic functions seems to be innate and predetermined for over 90% of us (Geshwind & Galaburda, 1986) but at the same time the development of normal cerebral dominance is dependent on the acquisition of language during critical childhood periods. If language is not acquired at the critical time, cerebral dominance is not established (Corballis, 1983). Congenitally deaf children and adults who have no language, including sign language, show no evidence of hemispheric specialization, while those deaf individuals who had acquired either vocal or sign language in childhood do show normal cerebral dominance (Curtiss, 1985). In the absence of established cerebral dominance, the hemispheres are relatively plastic for functional specialization. For example, if the left hemisphere is totally removed in infancy, before language acquisition, the right hemisphere can develop language function to a high level of competence. The plasticity of the right hemisphere is inversely related to the degree of left cerebral dominance. After normal cerebral dominance is fully established around the age of puberty, the right hemisphere is no longer able to achieve language competence.

Thus far, we have used the term "cerebral dominance" in its conventional static, though loose, definition, which does not address the question of interhemispheric forces. The term is used interchangeably with "cerebral laterality," denoting only that one or the other hemisphere has a superior capacity to acquire certain skills (Gazzaniga, 2000). Our concept is dynamic, with a broad connotation of cerebral dominance as a governing force involving neural stimulation and inhibition under the direction of a mental agency acting through a local anatomical substrate. Thus, cerebral dominance is not simply a neural specialization of a brain region for speech, handedness, or spatial orientation, but is a directional force serving mental unity. It is the force by which the mental activity of the brain is orchestrated by the verbal hemisphere.

The loss of cerebral plasticity in the right hemisphere is due to disuse and atrophy and/or inhibition imposed by cerebral dominance. This disuse might be due as much to a passive lack of stimulation rather than active inhibition, but it is as if the language areas in their imposition of cerebral dominance generate an "inhibitory tonus" of some form.

Our hypothesis is that in the savant syndrome there is an impaired cerebral dominance due to injury, disease, or maldevelopment of the verbal brain and therefore, less disuse and/or inhibition of the natural nonverbal ability of the mind. This becomes manifest in the seemingly extraordinary savant talents. These talents seem so extraordinary only because normally they are inhibited by the verbal brain. The liberated nonverbal facilities that are freed from the constraints of cerebral dominance reveal the natural capacity of the mind that is normally sacrificed to the tyranny of dominance. These capacities include thought and imagery that is nonunitary, parallel, and simultaneous, all of which is inconsistent with the primary tasks of the verbal mind. These are the capacities, however, that make it possible to do lightening processing of large amounts of data and to use instantaneous and simultaneous display of extensive eidetic imagery, the central elements involved in the savant talents.

In normal development, these ego dystonic capacities gradually wane until they can no longer be accessed. There are probably exceptional cases in which these talents are preserved even in the presence of normal cerebral dominance, and this is probably so in the case of true genius. The preservation of these talents would probably involve one or both of two factors: the early use of the talents and/or a diminished inhibition of them. Both of these seem to be true in many individuals regarded as geniuses. Mozart, for example, may have accessed these talents very early through his precocious musical ability, and there seemed to be less inhibition of the output of his nonconscious mind, as evidenced by his frequently experiencing a fully formed composition emerging mysteriously into consciousness (Abell, 2000). A diminished inhibition of these talents may occur in exceptional individuals who have anomalous patterns of cerebral laterality as, for example, when both hemispheres share dominance for language. In such cases, one would expect the inhibitory effects to be diminished or nullified.

Our hypothesis is that in the savant syndrome there is a dual mental organization and diminished inhibition—the impaired dominant verbal hemisphere and the disinhibited nonverbal hemisphere. This duality mimics some cases of dissociative disorder and suggests that

15

dialogue between the mental organizations might promote language acquisition by the originally nondominant hemisphere. The nondominant brain tissue should retain a higher plasticity and therefore a higher potential capacity for language acquisition even beyond the age of puberty. It might be possible to develop cerebral dominance and speech in the previously nonverbal hemisphere of a person with savant syndrome. This might result in normal manifested intelligence. However, it is predictable that this would mean the sacrifice of the savant talents, as those talents come under the inhibitory influence of the newly dominant and newly verbal hemisphere.

Cerebral dominance is relinquished during the course of the Instinctual Trauma Response. Perceptions continue to be registered and stored in the nonverbal mind but they are not verbally coded and therefore lack the context of sequence and time. If these memories are evoked later, the associated feelings of the experience may intrude into consciousness and be attributed to present events.

We believe that it is the relinquishing of cerebral dominance and the storage of perceptions without verbal coding that underlies traumatic dissociation. When memories are stored and held devoid of verbal narrative context, they are referred to as "dissociated memories."

## Dissociated memory

We contend that dissociated memory is a record of perceptions and experience that has not been coded as verbal narrative. Stern (2009) refers to this as "unformulated experience." Dissociated memory exists side by side with conscious memory and with repressed memory. Flashbacks that intrude into consciousness arise from dissociated images that are stored in a mental realm (the nonverbal mind) quite differently from that of repressed memory (the verbal mind).

Because both hemispheres of the brain store memory, with the left hemisphere usually processing information verbally, while the right stores images nonverbally, people are double-minded in their memory. A person comprehends every experience from two different points of view simultaneously and stores the memories separately. Normally, when we try to remember past events we tap into the verbal memory system and recover only the events that were verbally encoded and stored in the "explicit" or "declarative" system. We are normally unaware of the nonverbal "implicit" memory system that also holds a record of the events (Coltheart, 1989; Scaer, 2005). The implicit system stores images that are usually unavailable to the verbal probes of the conscious mind. This system has been studied in a variety of ways, including "priming" of word associations (Schacter, 1985) and recovery of learning during surgical anesthesia (Gopnik, 1993; Mashour, 2008).

Nonverbal encoding is already well established at birth. Once the child begins to use language, nonverbal memory runs parallel to verbal memory, but its retention is effortless (Parkin, 1989) and image-based (which includes timeless states of mind and body). It continues to function despite conditions that interfere with verbal memory such as anesthesia (Tinnin, 1994), sedation, or altered states of consciousness. And, most germane to our present concerns, it continues to record experience while the stream of consciousness is interrupted during a trauma.

Because so few people can think back and remember their lives as infants when experience was not verbally comprehended, many people have come to believe there is an innate "infantile amnesia." We believe this is a misunderstanding that is based on the belief that memory is solely the property of a unitary, verbal mind. Images of preverbal traumatic experiences that occurred before the emergence of language at age two or three are just as lasting and vivid as are memories of adult traumas that recur in flashbacks. Very early memories are more global and diffuse, lacking in figure/ground discrimination and constituted by visceral kinesthetic imagery as well as visual imagery. They may be more difficult to recognize in flashbacks, but the quality of urgency and danger can be as extreme as in the reenactment of adult trauma.

Dissociated traumatic images occupy this nonverbal realm and share the properties of effortless and timeless retention (Dell, 2009). Repressed memories, on the other hand, have the properties of explicit memory, that is, effortful retention and verbal encoding. Reversing repression requires ending that effort. Reversing dissociation requires active measures to gain access and imbue verbal coding to memory.

# Trauma and the Dual Brain

## Animal survival strategy

Being trapped in a dangerous situation evokes a pattern of innate physiological reflexes that can be understood as evolutionary survival strategies. The most primitive reflex is the freeze state. This was the primary survival strategy for early reptiles. The cold-blooded lizard could escape a predator by diving to the bottom of the water and remaining there until the predator gave up and went hunting elsewhere. The reptile's freeze was a prolonged torpor (Hofer, 1970) that slowed the breathing, reduced the heart rate, and lowered core body temperature.

Over evolutionary time, mammals acquired the escape strategy of explosive flight or fight but never lost the ancient freeze, as risky as it might be to warm-blooded creatures. Thus, when escape by fight or flight is thwarted, a mammal collapses into a freeze state and seems dead. If that mammal survives the brief state of torpor it may escape when the predator fails to complete the kill and chases another prey. According to Robert Scaer:

> *When fleeing and fighting are no longer physically possible, and the prey animal is in a state of helplessness, it will frequently enter the freeze, or immobility state, a totally instinctual and unconscious reflex. This behavior is common in most species including insects, reptiles, birds, and mammals. Since most such reflexes have evolved as a means of perpetuating the species, the freeze response is clearly of critical importance for survival (Scaer, 2001, p.16).*

## Human survival strategy

The human brain retains the neural apparatus for the reptilian freeze and the mammalian fight/flight survival strategy. The modern first-line human strategy was made possible by the acquisition of language. A person uses deliberate wiles, deception, and strategic planning—all capacities made possible by linear, sequential, and contextual thought. The structure of this conscious thought is language with its linear grammar involving subject, verb, and object. This structure proves fragile under severe stress. When survival is threatened and the person cannot devise a way out, the verbal mind gives way to the instinctive animal mind and its spurt of flight/fight action fueled by adrenalin. When that mammalian strategy fails and there seems to be no escape, the person may lapse into a reptilian freeze.

## The instinctual human response to trauma

Animals and humans respond to threatening events with evolutionary survival patterns that include startle, flight, fight, freeze, submission, and recuperative states, which involve wound care and gradual return to daily activities (Nijenhuis, Vanderlinden, & Spinhoven, 1998; Van der Hart, Nijenhuis, & Steele, 2006). The more recently acquired evolutionary patterns are elicited first and when escape is blocked they yield to the more primitive behaviors with the last-ditch effort representing the reptilian freeze state.

The first instinctual response usually begins with a startle, a brief and intense experience that shocks the individual into vigilance. Despite being extremely alert with attention locked on the threatening stimulus, the human's rational thinking begins to wane. The mammalian instinct for survival takes over, and the stress hormones (adrenalin and cortisol primarily) surge in readiness for fight or flight. When the person is trapped and all hope for escape is thwarted, rational thinking fails and the person surrenders to a stupefied freeze state, numb and motionless at first. Often, a parallel altered state of consciousness develops while the freeze persists. The person's awareness and perceived location of consciousness may shift to deep in the body or somewhere outside the body. The body now may behave like a mesmerized slave in automatic obedience. The person's detached perception may temporarily be protected from the pains of the body, but these unverbalized experiences may later become unspeakable body memories. Finally, when the immediate threat is past and verbal thought and body awareness return, the victim can attend to wounds and begin self-repair.

| The components of the Instinctual Trauma Response |
|---|
| • Startle |
| • Attempts to fight or flee |
| • Freeze |
| • Altered state of consciousness |
| • Automatic obedience (submission) |
| • Self-repair |

Any one of these may emerge as symptoms in the aftermath of trauma. The major cause of subsequent symptoms is due to the freeze state itself along with the failure of verbally coded thought.

## Pre-callosal, preverbal trauma

When Lou was in his medical internship in 1961, he was taught that the reaction of babies to seemingly painful stimuli was simply reflexive and devoid of thought or memory. One of his first patients in pediatrics was a three-day-old girl who underwent major abdominal surgery for pyloric stenosis requiring a resection of her stomach. She was securely restrained and—as was the practice of the time with infants—the surgery was done without pain control. Pancuronium, a curare-type paralyzing drug, was administered. She collapsed into immobility and gave the appearance of being anesthetized. She could not fight the intubation of a respiratory tube into her windpipe, and her protest must have been converted to an instinctual freeze. After surgery, the freeze state returned in episodes of unresponsiveness. This persisted for a few days, and it seemed she might die. Finally, she revived and became able to take milk from a bottle and hold it down.

The medical staff considered this a success. We now believe that if that baby girl lived and was seen today as a fifty-year-old woman, she would likely give a history of life-long neuroticism, heightened vulnerability to trauma, and would possibly present with complex PTSD or dissociative disorder.

As we will discuss, traumatic experiences that occur later, after cerebral dominance is established, have in common a traumatic loss of cerebral dominance and an emergent freeze state during which the survival instincts do not become verbally coded. This recapitulates the brain state of the preverbal period. During the preverbal period, there is no cerebral dominance and no verbal coding. Memory of adverse experiences is held in images and sensations without words. When this memory is later triggered, the fear and pain may be experienced as if in the present. Preverbal memories of adverse events or conditions (such as neglect or isolation) do not find closure. Narrative closure requires verbal narrative. Survival instincts that are activated during infancy can continue as unfinished business throughout life.

## Premature ego formation

Another reason that adverse experiences during the preverbal period can be so disturbing throughout life is the premature maturation that may accompany a child's struggle for survival. The early psychoanalysts wrote about premature ego development in psychopathology (Mahler, Pine, & Bergman, 1975). Recently, clinicians have looked at this from the point of view of attachment theory (Schore, 2000). We understand premature maturation to be the formation of preverbal *latent mental systems* organized around survival instincts, often referred to as parts or ego states (Watkins & Watkins, 1979). These latent mental organizations persist into the verbal period following callosal maturation as nonconscious parts of the emerging personality. They may give rise to compelling emotions and behavior patterns or an urgent attachment cry of fear and isolation. Goulding and Schwartz (2002) refer to them as problematic "exiles" residing deep within a person's system of subconscious parts.

## Governing mental system after callosal maturation

Once the two brains are communicating via the maturing corpus callosum, the language hemisphere becomes dominant and assumes ownership and direction of mental reflection, intention, will, behavior, speech, and even emotion. Thus emerges the governing mental system and the individual's illusion of unity (Tinnin, 1990). The governing mental system is commonly referred to as the Ego, and in terms of the structural theory of dissociation as the Apparently Normal Personality (Van der Hart, et al., 2006). However, we posit that normal verbal consciousness is limited by its symbolizing nature and its sense of unitary agency. Verbal consciousness is deaf to the nonverbal mind.

The structure of verbal consciousness is determined by the linear (spatialized) logic and grammar of language. The self is experienced as a unitary agent (subject) acting (verb) on the environment (object) over time (tense). The storage of information in long-term memory requires verbal symbolization and narrative structure. The relation of consciousness to language is much debated. An excellent summary is found in Steven Pinker's *The Stuff of Thought: Language as a Window into Human Nature* (Pinker, 2008).

## The quadrune mind and vulnerability of consciousness

An evolutionary approach to the study of the brain reveals that brains of advanced mammals comprise three main parts that in their structure and chemistry reflect developments identified with reptiles, early mammals, and late mammals. This "triune" organization described by Paul MacLean (1990) led to our understanding of the instinctual survival responses observed in humans today. These are the reptilian freeze, the early mammalian flight/flight, and the neomammalian evasive reactions to threat. What we term the human Instinctual Trauma Response is best understood in terms of a "quadrune" brain organization, which includes verbal consciousness as the uppermost and most recently acquired part. This concept places two inconspicuous language areas of the left hemisphere—Wernicke's area in the left temporal lobe and Broca's area a bit distant in the left parietal lobe—atop the schematic depicting the quadrune brain. The remaining divisions are stacked in the order of evolutionary phases of development: neomammalian nonverbal thought, paleomammalian fight/flight, and at the bottom, reptilian freeze.

The most recently acquired brain systems are the most vulnerable to survival threats. For example, the brain system most involved in verbal consciousness is the first to be affected by anesthesia. The anesthetized patient may appear to be sound asleep, while in fact, the nonverbal brain remains alert to the voices of the surgical team, the body's paralysis, and to the surgeon's scalpel. Finally, unable to escape by fight or flight, the patient's brain may yield to the freeze instinct.

Verbal consciousness is able to relinquish cerebral dominance under nontraumatic circumstances. It may happen in a peak experience that brings an expansive feeling of oneness with all. Transcendent experiences of love or spirituality probably involve relinquishing cerebral dominance. The induction of hypnosis or various approaches for desired altered states of consciousness involve relinquishing of dominance. Such experiences will not result in post-traumatic symptoms if survival instincts are not aroused. However, in traumatic experiences, when the threat to survival is overwhelming, the relinquishing of consciousness will generate timeless experiences of danger frozen in dissociated memory.

We contend that the crux of trauma is the instinctual survival response of a freeze state that follows a thwarted fight/flight response. The event that will traumatize a person is one in which the victim is trapped and lapses into a freeze. At this point, the nonverbal survival instincts have usurped the verbal governing mental system and its brain dominance. The brain has reverted to its more primitive animal nature. Outwardly, the person may appear stunned and show varying degrees of torpor from mild slowing to full paralysis. Inwardly, thinking and self-awareness can be drastically changed. One might feel numb and outside of one's body and feel that the experience is timeless. As the freeze state wanes, it may become an experience of automatic obedience. Finally, as recovery begins, the body regains feeling of the pains and sensations not attended to earlier. Then, wound care and grief begin.

## *Clinical Consequences of Trauma*

### Type 1 and Type 2 trauma

The major forms of post-traumatic disorders fit on a continuum from acute stress disorder to dissociative identity disorder. On that continuum lie post-traumatic stress disorder (PTSD), complex PTSD, dissociative PTSD (those with PTSD who experience auditory hallucinations without schizophrenia) (Holmes & Tinnin, 1995), and a variety of dissociative disorders (Figure 1). The cause

23

of those conditions on the left of the continuum are episodic traumas, usually single events, termed Type 1 traumas, while the Type 2 traumas on the right result from prolonged repetitive trauma such as child abuse or adult captivity (Herman, 1992; Terr, 1991).

Type 1 trauma catches the victim off-guard and is usually sudden and catastrophic. The altered state of consciousness is often a stunned shock. There are many kinds of Type 1 traumas. Even painful medical procedures or surgery or any frightening condition involving changing states of consciousness may constitute Type 1 traumas. A loss of consciousness under fearful conditions such as a head injury or anesthesia in which the tougher nonverbal mind ticks right along while the verbal brain fades may result in post-traumatic symptoms.

Type 2 traumas are usually expected, although unavoidable. The child who is chronically sexually abused has learned what to expect and may automatically lapse into a freeze and an altered state for self-protection. During prolonged and repeated altered states, in the default of normal consciousness, a substitute "will" sometimes develops to protect the helpless body. These substitute intentional states will be dissociated when normal consciousness resumes (Tinnin, 1990) and they may remain as latent mental systems. Their mental activity continues during that latency and may range from simple reflexive volition to a stream of thought that may be perceived by the person as auditory hallucinations. These latent states may stay quiescent or actively compete for consciousness. It is Type 2 trauma in early childhood that usually leads to dissociative identity disorder (Herman, 1992).

## The core post-traumatic symptoms

People will react to all kinds of trauma, whether Type 1 or Type 2, with a remarkably similar core group of symptoms. The triad of post-traumatic effects are: reenactment, in which traumatic images intrude into consciousness; numbing phenomena and diminishing involvement in the external world; and an arousal state that accompanies the attitude of dire expectancy.

# THE SPECTRUM OF TRAUMA-RELATED DISORDERS

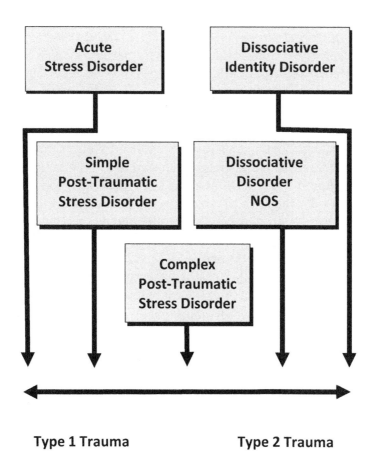

Figure 1

Verbal symbolization supports the conscious sense of a unitary "I" that acts with willful volition and thinks in a logical (linear) sequence. The verbal mind normally leads the thinking of the nonverbal mind and establishes the mental context of time, place, and will. The nonverbal mind normally operates with an automatic "followership" with unquestioning acceptance of the verbal dictates. During infancy, before verbal cerebral dominance is established, and then later, whenever verbal dominance is interrupted (for example, during anesthesia or a traumatic altered state of consciousness), the nonverbal mind is leaderless. Without verbal leadership, the nonverbal mind lacks a unitary "I" or a sense of linear causality and sequential experience. Without verbal context, the nonverbal mind must rely on "primary process" thinking (Arieti, 1976), and the stored images may be experienced as occurring in the present instead of being narrative and historical.

### Reenactment

Reenactment can be subtle, as in the sensations of body memories, or terrifying in the re-experiencing of emotion felt in the traumatic event. The symptoms may be dramatic, as in a flashback when the person behaviorally relives a trauma. Specific phases of the trauma response may be triggered by certain stimuli, and the person may behave accordingly. For example, the state of automatic obedience that followed a sexual assault might be triggered by contemporary threats or commands of another person. The same holds for outbursts, rages, fleeing with no apparent reason, and some obsessive-compulsive rituals. The individual usually shows an obligatory and automatic rationalization of the intrusive behavior as related to the present situation without insight into the reenactment. Reliving of traumas may occur in flashbacks, trance states, and nightmares.

### Numbing

Post-traumatic numbing in the form of alexithymia (involving the loss of conscious connection to the emotions) poses a major obstacle to treatment approaches that depend on emotional expression. Traumatized individuals suffer both emotional and physical numbing. One's pain threshold may be increased and visual fields diminished, sometimes resulting in tunnel vision. They may deliberately cut themselves to draw blood or burn themselves to induce pain and dispel their deadening anesthesia. Post-traumatic numbing of emotional attachment to others results in estrangement, divorce, and social withdrawal, sometimes to the extent of becoming a recluse or hermit.

### Arousal

Arousal symptoms complete the symptom triad. As long as there are dissociated traumatic memories, the individual experiences an aroused expectancy of a dire outcome. One's body tenses and braces against the blow. There is a sense of danger from within (in the form of intrusive images) and from without in the dread of being trapped or destroyed, so the person is forever vigilant. Sleep is feared because of the repeated reliving of the trauma in nightmares. The traumatized person stays tensed for action, and the flashback is triggered by unexpected stimuli.

## Complications of trauma

### Victim mythology and neuroticism

People who have suffered early childhood trauma or repetitive trauma in later years nearly always have an unhappy view of themselves and their future. They often develop a pessimistic worldview that they hold with conviction. They feel increasingly vulnerable as if permanently damaged and weakened by the trauma. They feel diminished and no longer able to function on a level with others. The sense of being handicapped may result in an unwillingness to participate socially with other people. At the same time, there is a fear that the outside world is so hostile and dangerous that the most one can hope for is to simply survive. The motto becomes "Safety first."

These pessimistic attitudes constitute the post-traumatic mentality that is referred to as *victim mythology*. The same set of attitudes make up the so-called trait of *neuroticism,* which is recognized as a precursor of depression and many other mental illnesses. The term neuroticism was coined by Hans Eysenck and measured by tests that he and his wife developed (H.J. Eysenck, & B.G. Eysenck, 1975). The questionnaires measure anxiety, guilt, low self-esteem, tension, moodiness, hypochondria, lack of autonomy, and obsessiveness. We view victim mythology and neuroticism as identical in traumatized individuals.

## Dissociative attention deficit

Another complication of trauma is dissociative states. A common form is a state of confusion in a person whose distractibility and forgetfulness may appear to be willful inattention. We have seen this in persons with severe, chronic trauma from child abuse and in war veterans with combat trauma. A consequence of extensive trauma is the experience of multiple concurrent streams of thought that relate to chronically aroused survival instincts. The individual's stream of consciousness is repeatedly interrupted, sometimes so much so that the person cannot follow simple conversation. These fixed states intrude into ongoing conscious thought.

The observer sees the failure of attention first. When we worked with combat veterans in art therapy groups we found that we had to give simple instructions repeatedly. It took time and patience to learn from the veterans that they experienced streams of thought that they could not suppress while trying to carry out tasks. Children with attention deficit disorder and hyperactivity report racing thoughts. It may not be clear when this is a dissociative phenomenon arising from competing streams of thought. The adults with combat PTSD were usually not hyperactive. Those with the more severe attention problems were hypoactive and emotionally numb.

## Dissociative splitting

The phenomenon of splitting is a form of dissociation that has been understood as an ego defense designed to reduce anxiety by simplifying the world and self into the two categories of good and bad. Splitting is an unfortunate term because it implies that there was once something whole that is now divided. The splitting phenomenon is the separation of mutually contradictory, alternately conscious mental states. Otto Kernberg (1976) referred to these as independent "ego states" involving "repetitive, temporally ego-syntonic, compartmentalized psychic manifestations." He, however, viewed these as a "regressive transference reaction in which a specific internalized object relationship was activated in the transference." This formulation overlooked the fact that the patient switches between different states of mind, with each state disowning the other, often with little memory transfer between them. The patient shifts from extreme devaluation to idealization of self and others. When in one polarized mental state, the individual may show an indifference to the previous mental state or even amnesia for it. The patient abruptly reverses actions, decisions, and commitments, suddenly breaking relationships, only to mend them the next day.

In our experience, dissociative splitting is seen in individuals who were severely neglected, battered, or sexually abused as infants or toddlers. Many of these people merit the diagnosis of borderline personality disorder and show extreme instability of emotion and behavior.

### Auditory hallucinations

More severe forms of dissociation include hallucinated internal voices, the so-called "command hallucinations" in which the voice reveals an independent will that may be turned against the person. We found hallucinations to be present in two-thirds of combat veterans with PTSD (Holmes & Tinnin, 1995) and in forty percent of our civilian PTSD patients. It was the spouses of the veterans who alerted us to the dissociative nature of PTSD ("I swear that monster he becomes is not my husband.") The most obvious and extreme form of dissociation occurs in people with dissociative identity disorder who experience alter personalities that compete for dominance.

### Dissociative disorders

Almost half of the patients in our clinic were diagnosed with dissociative disorders. Ten percent had dissociative identity disorder. These high rates are to be expected in a trauma center. Others have reported prevalence rates among psychiatric inpatients of 18.9% for dissociative disorder and 4.4% for dissociative identity disorder (Friedl, Draijer, & DeJonge, 2000 as reported by Nijenhuis, Van der Hart, and Steele, 2002). Many of these patients had been battered as children, and their chronic traumatization often began in infancy. Their clinical presentation is highly varied and they are often diagnosed with schizophrenia or bipolar disorder. Many were diagnosed as borderline personality disorder along with a variety of DSM-IV Axis I disorders (American Psychiatric Association, 1994).

## Altered states of consciousness

An altered state of consciousness is experienced in hypnotic trances, transcendental meditation, anesthesia, out-of-body experiences, near-death experiences, and in many other conditions, as well as during a traumatic experience. The mental mechanism of altered states involves a diffusion of the self, or ego, boundary. With ego boundary diffusion, one loses the fundamental self-regulating functions that include identity, subjective time, volition, body image, verbal symbolization, and reality monitoring. The loss of these functions accounts for much of the subjective experience of an altered state of consciousness.

## Dissociative regression

When a dissociative state is extended in time or when these states are repetitive, it becomes increasingly difficult for the individual to recover. Dissociative regression sets in, resulting in a condition of helpless confusion and dependency. Dissociative regression makes it impossible for the patient to respond to conventional verbal therapies and it requires a reality-based, hands-on intervention (Gantt, 1979a). We describe this approach in *Treatment Methods, Phase 1,* below.

# PART 2: ASSESSMENT AND TREATMENT METHODS

## *Assessment*

### Taking a trauma history

Our modern methods of treating the consequences of trauma make it possible to expect full recovery in most patients with PTSD and almost as high a percentage in dissociative disorders (Gantt & Tinnin, 2007). Of course, this will hold only for those treatment methods that address the etiology of post-traumatic disorders, which means addressing the causative traumas. The methods herein that are based on dual brain dynamics employ sequential trauma processing beginning with foundational preverbal trauma. Taking a thorough trauma history is key to successful treatment. The earliest traumas have the greatest effect on psychopathology. Our template for a trauma time-line (Figure 2) is skewed to the left so that some 50% of the lifetime trauma weight occurs before age 8 as shown in this scale:

## EXAMPLE OF A TRAUMA TIME-LINE

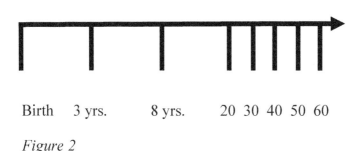

Birth    3 yrs.        8 yrs.        20 30 40 50 60

*Figure 2*

The first trauma time-line a patient draws is rarely complete. People usually remember additional important events as they process known traumas. The trauma time-line helps to understand the burden of trauma on one's life.

## Evaluation for PTSD and dissociative disorders

When most patients try to explain and account for all of the past symptoms, they may make no mention of traumatic experiences. Written questionnaires along with a verbal interview help. However, crucial traumas may be forgotten, and the critical preverbal traumas elude verbal probes. It is most helpful if family members can describe the patient's birth, early illnesses, and surgeries. The clinician assembles as full a picture as possible of preverbal adverse childhood events and attachment problems.

The trauma profile we have assembled is a set of self-administered questionnaires used to gauge the extent of regression, dissociation, alexithymia, general psychiatric symptoms, and severity of post-traumatic symptoms. This includes a six-item test for ego regression that we devised and named the *Dissociative Regression Scale (DRS)* (Tinnin & Gantt, 2000, p. 83). The profile also includes the *Dissociative Experiences Scale (DES)*, a twenty-eight-item scale that is widely used to screen for post-traumatic disorders (Bernstein & Putnam, 1986). The *Symptom Checklist-45 (SCL-45)* (Alvir, Schooler, Borenstein, Woerner, & Kane, 1988) is used to measure global distress. We use the *Toronto Alexithymia Scale (TAS)* (Taylor, Bagby, Ryan, Parker, Doody, & Keefe, 1988) because we find the reversal of alexithymia (Appel & Sifneos, 1979) to be a good measure of recovery after treatment. The *Impact of Event Scale (IES)* (Horowitz, Wilner, & Alvarez, 1979) measures the PTSD intrusive and avoidant symptoms. We use the trauma profile to measure change over time as well as for initial evaluation.

These questionnaires are not suitable for children. There are some promising scales for PTSD and dissociative disorders being developed by others, and we hope to assemble trauma profiles for children and adolescents in the near future.

*[See additional "Notes on Recommended Assessments" at the end of the references.]*

## Interpretation

In our clinical experience, we see the Dissociative Experiences Scale as influenced somewhat by the severity of symptomatic distress and by the degree of regression. Without extreme symptoms or regression (that is, a SCL-45 below 100 and a DRS score lower than the DES score), a DES score in the range of 20 to 30 suggests a diagnosis of PTSD. DES scores of 30 to 50 suggest dissociative disorder, not otherwise specified (DDNOS), and 50 or more usually indicates dissociative identity disorder (DID).

On the other hand, if the SCL-45 exceeds 100 or the patient is regressed as indicated by the DRS score being higher than the DES, then higher DES scores will occur than have been reported with these diagnostic categories. PTSD will likely be associated with an elevated DES in the 30-40 range, while the 40-60 range suggests DDNOS, and above 60, DID.

We find the TAS is nearly always elevated in chronic or severe post-traumatic conditions. It is a good indicator of complete recovery following treatment when the score falls below 70.

The DRS is not standardized but it has been useful for estimating regression. It uses the same format as the DES and requires a DES value for a baseline. That is, when it is first administered to a patient, it is given along with the DES, and the scores are compared.

## Criteria for recovery

We establish criteria for recovery when we do the initial diagnostic evaluation. The usual criteria include:

- o Presenting problems resolved (for example, intrusive, avoidant, arousal symptoms, depersonalization, derealization, disturbances of consciousness or memory)
- o DES<20, SCL-45<80, TAS<74
- o Amelioration of suicidal urges and hallucinations
- o Reliable emotional stability
- o Participation in all chosen significant activities

## Follow-up testing

We schedule follow-up testing with the trauma profile for one week, three months, and six months after termination.

## The Formal Elements Art Therapy Scale (FEATS)

This measure uses a standardized drawing task [The "Draw a Person Picking an Apple from a Tree" (PPAT)] designed to assess clinical state and change over time. The PPAT is measured with the Formal Elements Art Therapy Scale (FEATS) (Gantt & Tabone, 1998). Specific materials are used for this task [white drawing paper 12 by 18 inches and a 12-color set of "Mr. Sketch" ™ scented markers]. Materials other than these invalidate the comparison with other samples. This drawing is repeated in the termination session. If the patient gives consent, the pictures are scored and held for use in our outcome studies.

## Evaluation for dual-brain pathology in chronic disease states

There is an astounding correlation between early childhood trauma and the occurrence of the most common and severe chronic illnesses (physical and mental) as shown by the Adverse Childhood Experiences study (Felitti, et al., 1998). The underlying physiological and neurological mechanisms that relate adverse childhood events to adult illness remain a matter of conjecture. Our hypothesis involves traumatic dissociation in which latent mental systems or "parts" are generated during the Instinctual Trauma Response and remain active although outside of consciousness. These instinctual survival patterns of activity tend to blend into conscious behavior and influence a person's decisions and viewpoints while also influencing the internal homeostasis of the body. The influence of dissociated parts may expose a person to known risk factors for chronic disease such as smoking, obesity, promiscuity, and drug abuse. Below we discuss some clinical clues to detecting problematic latent mental systems.

### Recurring excess affect and inappropriate behavior

Dissociated parts may cause persisting emotional pain such as unexplained fearfulness, shame, guilt, or hypervigilance. They may be manifested also by impulsive or compulsive behaviors.

- *Case example*

*Dean was 26 years old when he turned to trauma therapy out of desperation due to his life-long problem of stress intolerance. He and his mother believed that his problems were caused by major surgery during infancy and later repeated painful medical procedures. They had found no physician understanding or agreement with this until they came to the trauma clinic.*

*Dean would switch from a sensitive, loving child to a tight-lipped, belligerent fighter when he felt physically trapped or threatened; it was as if there was a "second personality" that would scream, kick, and bite. This behavior began around two years of age. When he became mildly upset or irate, his parents were able to soothe him quite easily through touch and physical nurturing or talking. When he experienced a stressful situation and thought he was trapped, his affect became visibly different according to his mother. "His mouth becomes tight, he gets a belligerent facial expression, and his body becomes very rigid." It was then that he might run. As a child, his running would take him outside and away from the house. His flight from stress never ceased. He ran away from home while in high school, then from college to home, and from different jobs on four separate occasions, some in the middle of the night.*

*His childhood history explained his sensitivity to being trapped. His delivery at birth was unremarkable, but he could not nurse or take milk without choking. He was born with a congenital abnormality—a fistula opening between his esophagus and trachea. Whatever he swallowed might enter his windpipe. Immediate surgery was necessary. It is not known if anesthesia was used. The baby survived, but the post-operative scarring of the esophagus narrowed the aperture and threatened to block the passage of liquids or foods. The treatment for this required painful esophageal dilatations one to three times a week for about six months. Again, it is unknown if there was any pain control with these procedures. Until 1987 surgeons routinely did infant surgery without analgesia (Anand & Hickey, 1987). He*

35

*underwent surgery again at age four to repair his stomach valve. He had anesthesia for that surgery. He reports that when he awoke he "went crazy" and pulled out all of his tubes. Repeated evaluations and sometimes dilatations followed, and finally the lower third of his esophagus was removed because of the development of precancerous changes when he was fourteen.*

*During his 35 hours of marathon outpatient trauma therapy he processed the surgical traumas and gained contact and communication with a dissociated infant part of himself that was locked into a fight/flight instinctual response. When he found closure to the traumatic memories, the baby part was liberated from the burden of having to escape. Dean felt like a new man without the burden of fight/flight and the accompanying hypervigilance and distrust of others.*

## Whole-body symptoms

When dissociated parts are the consequence of preverbal trauma, the patient might complain of unrelenting whole-body pain or report attacks of air hunger or panic.

- *Case example*

*At age 43, Tressa was disabled due to her panic disorder, which was not controlled by a variety of medications prescribed over two years. Her panic attacks began after a traumatic experience at work. She was a night attendant at a motel when a robber threatened her at knifepoint. She managed to take flight and ducked into an equipment room where she crouched in the dark, listening for the robber. The robbery was thwarted by the entry of other people into the registration area. She was unhurt but she became phobic for the workplace and developed recurrent panic states.*

*Her need was urgent, and the trauma clinic focused on the immediate issue of the robbery trauma. She felt some relief, but the panic attacks continued. The focus of trauma processing shifted to her foundational traumas of severe neglect during infancy and sexual abuse as a toddler by her*

36

*mother's boyfriend. The key scene in her memory was hiding from him in a basement boiler room that was very much like her adult experience in the robbery. When she found closure to these memories the panic attacks ceased.*

### Small, intrusive behaviors: Tics, stuttering

Involuntary facial tics and stuttering are commonly the intrusive expressions of latent parts. Facial tics or involuntary grimaces that are not a part of Tourette's syndrome or other neurological disorders may arise from parts. Stuttering is sometimes an indicator of an intruding problematic part.

### Resistance to ordinary treatment

The symptomatic intrusions of latent mental systems are not likely to respond to ordinary treatment. Treatment resistance suggests the influence of post-traumatic latent mental systems.

- *Case example*

  *Thirty-year-old Janice complained of a generalized headache that was always present for as long as she could remember. Her present treatment began with processing her birth as a trauma and then processing severe neglect during infancy. It seemed to her that the only attention she got from her parents was when she fell off the sofa and injured her head. After that, she developed a pattern of repetitive head banging. Her treatment included an externalized dialogue (see the section on Treatment Methods) with a dissociated inner head-banging baby. When she unburdened the baby, her headache stopped.*

## Overview of Treatment

## Three primary tasks of trauma therapy

Unresolved trauma amounts to a continuing unfinished crisis. The dissociated traumatic memory involves continuing efforts by the dissociated self that was in the trauma to escape or survive or somehow to bring an end to the situation. Years later it is up the person's present self to access that memory, bring closure to it, and rescue the dissociated past self. A final step is often necessary to repair the person's trauma-based outlook on life. The three-step process to complete the treatment can be remembered as the three R's:

### 1. Render the traumatic memories fully conscious and historical (that is, as past tense)

The first step is to tell the story as a full narrative with a beginning, middle, and end. The narrative must contain both the narrative truth given by the person's verbal memory and understanding of the event and the story given by the nonverbal experience. The verbal narrative usually contains the life circumstances, the setting, the characters, and the script or action. The nonverbal story contains a parallel experience of body sensations arising from the innate survival instincts of startle, fight/flight, freeze, submission, automatic obedience, and self-repair of the Instinctual Trauma Response. The compound narrative brings closure to both the nonverbal and the verbal memories.

### 2. Repair the traumatic dissociation

This step rescues the traumatized self still locked in the timeless instinctual state. The externalized dialogue (described later) between the present self and the dissociated self makes it possible to repair the traumatic dissociation.

### 3. Relieve the burdens of victim mythology

Chronic trauma usually causes a pessimistic outlook on life. Underlying this outlook is an accumulation of trauma-based burdens carried by dissociated parts created in the traumatic experiences. An extension of the externalized dialogue, which we will describe as *parts work,* accomplishes the necessary unburdening.

## Objectives of trauma therapy

### Process the traumas sequentially

If the sequential trauma processing proceeds in chronological order beginning with the very earliest preverbal traumas, the three R's become easier and easier. The patient becomes more knowledgeable and finally, capable of using the treatment procedures independently.

### Complete the primary tasks

One major objective of trauma therapy is to process as many of the patient's traumas as possible. In the case of severely traumatized individuals, it may not be practical to complete the primary tasks— the three R's above—or all of the traumas in the time allotted for office treatment. However, the third objective will help make full recovery possible, even in the most severe cases.

### Provide tools for on-going self-help

The third objective, then, is to empower the patient to use the treatment tools for on-going self-help. These tools are the self-administered graphic narrative and the externalized dialogue. The patient learns how to do these procedures in the clinic and is now ready to do them at home. In summary, the three objectives of the treatment are to do sequential trauma processing, to complete the primary tasks, and to provide tools for on-going self-help.

## Phases of trauma therapy

### First phase: Treatment of dissociative regression and trauma phobia

There are three phases of treatment. The first phase involves treatment of any dissociative regression (described below) and management of the patient's trauma phobia. The first trauma processing of a preverbal trauma is designed to diminish trauma phobia. This relatively unthreatening procedure introduces the patient to the treatment methods and to the Instinctual Trauma Response.

### Second phase: Narrative trauma processing and repair of traumatic dissociation

The second phase is the narrative processing of the traumatic memories and repair of the traumatic dissociation. It may be relatively brief in simple PTSD, requiring six to twelve hours. In the more complex PTSD or dissociative disorders, the processing of each primary trauma usually requires more time.

### Third phase: Parts work

The third phase is less structured and more variable from patient to patient. This is devoted to the repair of victim mythology and parts work. The major emphasis is on the patient's identification of dissociated parts, communication and negotiation with those parts, and on establishing a secure integrated system of parts under the leadership of the patient. The parts work (described below) repairs victim mythology by a process of unburdening protector parts.

## Goals of trauma therapy

### Cure rather than amelioration

These methods of trauma therapy are directed to the etiology of the post-traumatic condition. The goal of treatment is to cure the problem rather than to simply ameliorate it. Coping strategies alone serve only to put off dealing with the trauma, which must be done before full recovery will occur.

### Promote self-care and prevention of trauma

Our methods aim to repair the traumatic dissociation, integrate the parts, and promote self-care and prevention of future trauma. The patient learns to anticipate and ward off the instinctual responses to threats or to being trapped.

### Promote interhemispheric integration

Recovery means not only relief of symptoms but also an expansion of consciousness with greater access to normal emotion. In dual-brain terms this means promotion of cross-callosal exchange between the hemispheres.

## *Treatment Methods*

## Phase 1: Management of trauma phobia and dissociative regression

"Trauma phobia" is a term coined by Pierre Janet more than a hundred years ago (Van der Hart & Brown, 1992). It refers to a person's fearful reluctance to think about and talk about an unresolved trauma. It is an anxiety that increases as the trauma is approached in therapy but vanishes as soon as narrative closure to the traumatic memory is achieved. We believe that this anxiety is not about warded-off affect and it will not serve as a guide to the intensity of the traumatic emotion. Instead, it is related to the fear of reliving a trauma and losing one's sense of mental unity. It seems that the greater the organization of a dissociated complex (e.g., an ego state or alter personality), the greater the fear. Once someone processes a trauma safely and studies it in relation to the Instinctual Trauma Responses, he or she learns it is possible to process a traumatic memory without reliving it. Trauma phobia is not a reason to delay trauma work unless the person is experiencing dissociative regression. This state sometimes follows severe alterations of consciousness as in depersonalization or derealization or interruptions of consciousness by amnesia, dissociated memories, voices, or parts.

### Methods to reverse dissociative regression

In dual brain terms, dissociative regression is weakened cerebral dominance and a corresponding weakening of the autonomous ego functions. The fundamental verbal elements of consciousness (identity, volition, time, reality monitoring, self-image, and verbal symbolization) fail to support and orient the whole mind. As verbal dominance weakens, the individual's capacity for self-regulation diminishes. One's stimulus barrier weakens. The person becomes unable to manage ordinary tasks of daily living. The diurnal rhythm and sleep/wake cycles may be lost. Routine personal hygiene, self-care, social communication, and common sense may fail.

This state of cerebral dominance insufficiency is not depression. It is not a delirium or a toxic state and it does not respond to medication alone. The person must be helped by others to restore self-regulation. It is up to the therapist to orchestrate an organized effort to support and supervise the patient. Four objectives will guide this effort:

- *Provide a stimulus barrier*

Various psychotropic medications may be used for this purpose, but the primary thrust is to prescribe optimal mental stimulation with prohibitions against being in crowds or being alone, taking naps, drinking alcohol, or using drugs.

- *Reduce ambiguity*

The therapist assumes a directive role and prescribes the behavior of family members or others who will help care for the patient. The therapist makes the treatment agreement and the safety rules explicit, clear, and simple. Structured and unambiguous stimuli are needed to reduce regression.

- *Promote auxiliary ego function*

Significant others are recruited as therapeutic assistants to achieve the third objective, which is to provide any necessary auxiliary ego function by temporarily doing for the person what the person cannot do for himself or herself. This usually involves a "tough love" approach using firmness to keep the patient active and on task. The helper becomes an auxiliary ego for the patient by hands-on participation and assistance in household tasks. Completion of tasks is a potent corrective for regression, and the fact that it is a shared effort will not diminish its effectiveness.

- *Support self-regulation*

The autonomous ego functions include identity (the sense of self as an entity), volition (the exercise of will with intention and direction), time (sense of duration, sequence, past, and present), reality monitoring (distinguishing between fantasy and fact), body image (self boundary), and verbal symbolization (language function). The final objective is to support these functions. This can be accomplished with a daily schedule for sleep, meals, and activities, and the keeping of a daily log listing the time spent in all activities. This chore helps to repair the autonomous ego functions of time and volition. As the individual restores normal activities of daily life and attention to diet and goal-directed activity, those ego functions bounce back.

When the person becomes self-regulating and free of self-boundary diffusion, the regression regimen becomes redundant and the person can turn to narrative trauma processing.

- *Summary of anti-regression regimen*
  - Stimulus barrier
  - No crowds
  - No solitude
  - No naps
  - No alcohol or drugs
  - Reduction of ambiguity
  - Direction and prescription of behavior by therapist
  - Promotion of auxiliary ego function
  - Significant others as therapeutic assistants
  - Temporarily doing for the person what the person cannot do
  - "Tough love" approach
  - Support of autonomous ego functions
  - Use of daily log
  - Daily schedule for sleep, meals, and activities

*[See Appendix for forms to use in the anti-regression regimen.]*

## Methods to diminish trauma phobia

It is reassuring to the patient to learn about the hard-wired aspect of the Instinctual Trauma Response. When we show a video recording about it that includes a clip of an actor demonstrating its phases (Tinnin & Gantt, 1999), patients usually respond with recognition: "That's it! That's what it was like." The more familiarity patients gain with the instinctual survival states, particularly the near-death aspect of the freeze, the less the trauma phobia.

The most important preparation for trauma therapy is the experience of processing a non-threatening preverbal trauma. It can be a known traumatic experience or an imagined one. For example, the instruction given during guided imagery might be: "Picture yourself as an infant in diapers and in distress and describe what you see." With encouragement by the therapist, the patient narrates the visualized story beginning with the baby's startle and ending with the image of the baby recovered from the experience.

This is a practice for the later trauma processing to come. It introduces the patient to the goal of non-threatening and non-emotional trauma processing and to the use of an observer perspective to study the traumatic experiences. Patients often carry the expectation that trauma processing must involve reliving of the emotional experience. One's full realization that emotional reliving is not only unnecessary but undesirable will come with the experience of trauma processing.

- *Case example*

*At age 52, Dawn had been in treatment for thirty years for diagnoses of major depression, bipolar disorder, and PTSD. She had been taking antidepressant and antipsychotic medications for years. She believed the medications and psychotherapy helped her to avoid suicide and to continue working in clerical jobs, but her dark pessimism and fearfulness never relented. She felt it was her own fault. She explained that she was never able to talk about the incestuous abuse of her childhood. She trusted her current counselor but she still became panicked whenever she tried to talk about her trauma. Finally, she accepted the referral for intensive trauma therapy for a "last chance" effort.*

*Her evaluation revealed chronic depression, depersonalization, derealization, auditory hallucinations, and fearful hypervigilance but no evidence of thought disorder or paranoia. She was also free of regression. Her testing showed elevated levels of dissociation (DES=41), alexithymia (TAS=88), and symptoms of intrusion and avoidance (IES=59). The diagnostic impression was dissociative disorder, not otherwise specified (DDNOS).*

*The first treatment task was to reduce her trauma phobia. Despite her apprehension, she quickly grasped the concepts of the Instinctual Trauma Response and dissociation. She was willing to try the trauma processing of an imagined crib trauma. She understood that with the help of guided imagery she would visualize herself as a baby in diapers and in distress and that she would study the scene from the vantage point of an observer.*

*While being guided in her imagery, she imagined herself strolling along window-shopping in a friendly place. When she stopped and looked intently at an item behind the shop window, she followed instructions for liberating her inner Hidden Observer (a concept adapted from Hilgard, 1977) by stepping out of her body and looking at herself from the outside. As the Hidden Observer, she studied her body from several perspectives and when this imagery was accomplished she left her body there temporarily. The Hidden Observer pictured Dawn as a baby in diapers and in a crib. She watched and waited and finally saw the baby startled by loud arguing of her parents. She described a scene of the parents struggling against each other and pulling the baby between them. She saw the baby lapse into a freeze state before her father took her away from her mother and put her in a bedroom where she fell asleep.*

*As the Hidden Observer, Dawn remained impassive while viewing the scene. She was still calm during the imaginary return to the shop window and into her body. Upon arousing from her guided imagery trance, she was in deep thought about the event she had witnessed. She believed that the plight of the helpless baby pulled away by the father depicted the truth of her victimization. She knew now that she would fully face what had been her shameful secret, which she now sees as sexual abuse and captivity by her father.*

*When she completed the graphic narrative and listened to the therapist's re-presentation of the story, she avowed this as the story of her life from infancy to emancipation at sixteen. There was no more trauma phobia to prevent the trauma processing that followed.*

## Phase 2: Narrative trauma processing and repair of traumatic dissociation

What is important to know about the patient's traumatic experience? The *Diagnostic and Statistical Manual of Mental Disorders* (DSM-IV-TR) (American Psychiatric Association, 2000) tells us that first we must know if a trauma occurred. We learn that from the patient's story of a life-threatening event. For the event to qualify it must be of sufficient magnitude and it must sufficiently frighten the person. Many clinicians tell us that for treatment to proceed we must learn the meaning of the event for the person. Some claim that it is enough to find out the elicited ideas or cognitions or conditioned responses. These are all elements of a personal narrative; that is, what is said to have happened. Are they historically true, a record of what really happened? Or, are they perhaps an embellished concoction of truth, imagination, and fiction? What is fact and what is fiction and does it matter? If the person is honest, isn't the narrative truth sufficient?

No, the narrative truth is not sufficient. There is a nonverbal truth of the traumatic memory that is necessary for the therapeutic processing to achieve psychological closure to the memory. This nonverbal memory, which is not a part of what is said to have happened, is the basis of the core post-traumatic symptoms. The essence of the person's suffering is the unspoken trauma, which never became past tense. Psychological closure requires that the nonverbal story acquire a narrative structure with beginning, middle, and end.

The narrative truth of the person's story is achieved by words and sentences that convey information such as *who, what, when, and where*. The nonverbal truth is conveyed by the sensations of the body such as *startle, gasp, chest throbbing, limbs thrusting* (sensations of the adrenalin rush)*; sudden collapse, immobility, numbness, near-death perceptions of darkness and light* (sensations of the endorphin rush); *out-of-body perception, and wound-licking* (sensations of recovery). These sensations constitute the nonverbal memory. They are the effects of innate survival instincts, which we understand as the Instinctual Trauma Response (Gantt & Tinnin, 2009), a surge of evolutionary instincts activated in the nonverbal brain by the traumatic event.

The narrative truth is derived from the individual's story script. The nonverbal truth is known *a priori* as the hardwired automatic reaction to a traumatic event. It is the universal plot for every trauma story, be it combat trauma, abuse trauma, or medical trauma. In the course of treatment, it is translated into words and, when integrated into the verbal narrative, brought to closure and deposited into the long-term verbal memory bank. The individual now owns the compound narrative as a past event. It will no longer intrude into consciousness as unfinished business.

Granting that the nonverbal truth is necessary, one might ask "Is the narrative truth necessary?" So far, we have taken for granted that a verbal narrative with beginning, middle, and end is necessary. Our graphic narrative trauma processing is designed to fuse the verbal and nonverbal narratives. When we display the seven or more drawings that illustrate the trauma experience in accord with the phases of the Instinctual Trauma Response, we vocally *re-present* the story to the patient-as-audience. We narrate the verbal script organized according to the nonverbal plot and we promote the patient's avowal of the narrative as personal past history.

There are other methods to bring closure to the traumatic memory that do not require narrative and historical truth. EMDR, for example, might ask only for a focus on remembered emotions, as might some talk therapies. Some cognitive therapies deal with problematic thoughts. Some parts psychology approaches deal with unburdening of dissociated parts. Our own work with preverbal trauma may ask for an imagined narrative of an unremembered infant trauma and use that as a generic narrative truth to be integrated with the nonverbal truth of the Instinctual Trauma Response. Our processing of a known preverbal trauma asks for a verbal narrative that might be generated by guided imagery rather than conscious memory. We seek narrative truth but we cannot verify the story as historical truth.

We continue to rely on narrative truth, but how truthful the narrative is remains unknown. The following case illustrates this question.

- *Case example*

*At age 55 Laura was barely able to function and suffered constant burning pain around her genitals. The pain began at the time her infant daughter developed a severe diaper rash and Laura's application of medicated salve made the baby scream. Laura reacted with shock and revulsion toward her daughter and then had "flashes" of visual images of her mother burning her with cigarettes when she was a baby. Thus began her thirty years of faithfully attending counseling sessions (some group, mostly individual), plus taking medications with no relief from the pain.*

*In our one-week intensive trauma therapy program, she processed this trauma on the second day. In a light trance, she pictured her mother removing the diaper and deliberately burning the baby with a cigarette. She studied the baby's Instinctual Trauma Response while managing emotional detachment throughout. By the end of the day, she had drawn a graphic narrative of the trauma and witnessed a therapist re-presenting the drawn story. The processing closed with a successful video dialogue with the traumatized baby. Over the course of the intensive program her burning pain ceased entirely. She went on to process other important events also.*

*Originally, she had not believed her "flashes" to be true memory. The trauma therapists confirmed that the historical truth was unknown although she had processed what is known to be the "nonverbal truth" of a trauma. Some weeks after treatment Laura called with news that she had learned from a cousin that a friendly family member knew that Laura's mother actually committed the cigarette-burning.*

**Foundation trauma**

Most patients have a poor grasp of their true trauma burden. This is particularly true for the traumas of the newborn period and infancy. Not only are traumatic experiences of babies ubiquitous, they are foundational traumas that undermine a person's resilience. Fortunately, it is possible to diminish that pathology by at least one preverbal trauma processing that can provide a nonverbal template for reorganizing other traumas. That preverbal trauma may represent a foundation trauma that gives rise to later traumas or enters into later traumas. The following drawing (Figure 3) illustrates this as a fault in the foundation of a building that connects with visible later faults.

### Sequential trauma processing

As a general principle, it is best to process the earliest traumas first to avoid reactivating them by the work on later traumas. However, there are necessary exceptions to chronological processing in patients with urgent symptoms or certain dissociative disorders.

### An exception - PTSD with urgent symptoms

When one suffers traumatic grief, the underlying trauma may act to lock the bereavement in place, resulting in a frozen state of futility that prevents attention to any other trauma processing. The processing of this loss/trauma can free the person to turn to earlier traumas. The same problem may occur with post-disaster symptoms of unceasing flashbacks or flooding with catastrophic images. Phantom pain following amputation may demand immediate attention. In other cases, reenactment of the trauma can itself be life threatening. This can be the case with severe pseudo-seizures, organ shutdown in a fixed freeze state, extensive paralysis, or reenactments of a heart attack.

Once the presenting trauma is processed, it is wise to start again at the beginning to chronologically process foundation traumas. If there had been residual symptoms after processing an urgent trauma, they should now readily yield to a repeat processing.

- *Case example*

  *Frank was 46 years old when he was referred for treatment of his post-traumatic stress disorder that was diagnosed when he was seen on consultation as an inpatient in the University Hospital. He was being treated for complicated heart disease that had required repeated surgery, angioplasties, and multiple coronary catheterizations since the onset of severe angina and impending heart attack four years earlier.*

# FOUNDATION TRAUMAS

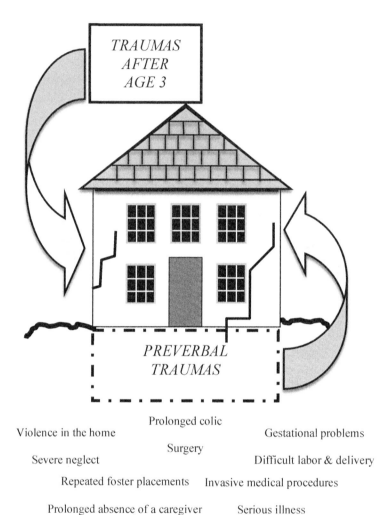

*Figure 3*

*He could not stop thinking about the first surgery and what he remembered of his heart attack. He was having flashbacks of chest pain day and night, and it was so frightening in his dreams that he was afraid to go to sleep. He feared he would die in his sleep. He was hypervigilant for physical signs of his expected death, and each pain was a dire alarm. His nerves were raw, and he exploded at those he loved. He felt he could not trust the doctors and was hopeless about his condition. He became dazed, distracted, and often sensed that his body did not belong to him and that he and the world were unreal. He constantly heard voices that he recognized were in his head but that he identified with friends or family members. The voices seemed benign in intent and they engaged in dialogue with him about trivial topics. He showed no evidence of a schizophrenic thought disorder, and his trauma profile scores were elevated (DRS=57, DES=63, TAS=76, SCL-45=139, IES=65) to the level usually seen with DDNOS.*

*Normally, we would have taken time to introduce Frank to the trauma therapy procedures and begin trauma processing with the earliest known traumas, but there was the obvious possibility that his repeated flashbacks might be lethal. He had already undergone fifteen cardiac catheterizations when his presentations in the emergency room were so convincing of repeated myocardial infarction. His reenactment of the original heart attack was not only psychological but also physiological. Even reenacted spasms of his coronary vessels could kill him. We elected to start with trauma processing of his heart attack, and he agreed with our recommendation.*

*The first trauma processing focused on the heart attack plus the emergency bypass surgery. Under hypnosis, Frank was able to recall the whole incident of the trauma including what happened before the ambulance arrived at his house, when he arrived at the hospital, and the whole heart bypass procedure while he was under anesthesia. He identified body memories of pressure, pain between his shoulder blades, coldness, discomfort with the table, pain with the electric shock to the heart muscle, and choking and suffocation due to the endotracheal tube in the recovery room. He stated that throughout the procedure he was afraid he would die. After the operation was over, he was afraid to sleep because he thought he would not be able to wake up.*

*He completed the graphic narrative processing, re-presentation, and externalized dialogue. His heart and surgical flashbacks ceased, so the urgency for treatment was relieved, but it became clear that he also had a multitude of earlier traumas that should be treated. He was able to safely revert to the usual chronological trauma processing.*

- ### *Certain dissociative states*

If a child or adult presents with severe dissociative attention deficit with or without hyperactivity, the related trauma (or attachment disturbance) is best addressed first. Suicidal command hallucinations are dangerous but can also be dealt with quickly (see below). A dissociative fugue state or amnesia will have to be treated before extensive trauma processing.

### Protocol for trauma processing

The procedures for accomplishing the first two primary tasks of trauma therapy are applied to each trauma in turn. The first task is narrative processing. This requires studying the traumatic event by imagery that evokes the right brain's nonverbal perceptions and subjects them to the left brain's verbal processing. (See *Narrative Processing* below.)

The second task repairs traumatic dissociation by the use of internal and externalized dialogue between the person in the present and the traumatized person in the trauma.

The third task of relieving victim mythology is introduced more gradually. It builds on the dialogue process for each trauma and the patient's developing realization of the influence that latent mental systems have on one's conscious outlook.

- *Begin with preverbal trauma processing*

Usually the first trauma to process is a preverbal trauma that happened in the first three years of life (but see above for exceptions to this rule). Examples of preverbal traumas include complicated birth, surgery (congenital heart malformations, pyloric stenosis), circumcision without anesthesia, colic, smothering, shaking, abuse, neglect, or separation from biological mother.

- *Case example*

*Twenty-four-year-old Nancy chose to process her birth by Caesarian section for her introduction to trauma processing by guided imagery. She responded well to the progressive relaxation and in the phase of visualization she succeeded in liberating a Hidden Observer by imagining stepping out of her body. As the Hidden Observer, she watched her newborn self being extracted through the incision in her mother's abdomen. Her mother was anesthetized and remained unconscious for an extended time. Nancy watched the baby react to the chill and bright light of the operating room, crying and screaming as she was being suctioned, weighed, and wrapped, finally lapsing into a freeze state of immobility. The baby was wheeled to the nursery before any contact with her mother's body. The Hidden Observer state did not fully protect Nancy from emotional response to what she saw, and she cried for the baby's shock of separation from her mother. She stayed with an effort to finally observe the gaze, so crucial to bonding but was unable to find it even when the baby was finally carried to her mother's hospital room. This presaged her subsequent study of a failure of attachment to her mother.*

**Generic preverbal trauma processing**

If there is no history of preverbal trauma, a generic preverbal trauma can be processed. We believe that a generic trauma narrative can serve as a template for the nonverbal narrative organizing of multiple preverbal traumatic experiences that may not be the object of the present narrative processing.

### Subsequent trauma processing

Following the preverbal trauma processing, there is usually less trauma phobia or other resistance to trauma work. The remaining known traumas are processed in turn. Not every traumatic experience must be processed. Events that are repetitions of the processed trauma can be skipped unless the intrusive symptoms persist.

### Narrative closure

The narrative processing of traumatic memory collects and organizes the nonverbal fragmented images and perceptions of the trauma into a coherent verbal structure with beginning, middle, and end. Now the person can assimilate the gathered fragments into verbal memory as personal history. The shock of the trauma is no longer stunning in present time and no longer felt as unfinished threat. The experience can finally be examined in the light of present consciousness as a remembered past event.

The assimilation of nonverbal images into verbal memory is promoted by participation of the "mind's eye." Imagery is a potent tool for the extraction and transformation of *memory shrapnel*. This is a term for fragments of the traumatic memory that seem to be out of context and that unexpectedly surface into awareness. There are several ways to recruit the mind's eye to the work of narrative processing. All of these methods depend on visual imagery to provide the narration, even though many of the memory fragments may not be visual. They may consist of bodily sensations such as pain or pressure or feelings of terror. Whatever the content, the nonverbal images can be detected by the mind's eye and reported.

### Verbal narrative processing using the Instinctual Trauma Response

It is exceedingly difficult to simply recite a traumatic experience. Festering memory fragments escape the verbal probes of conscious memory and block narrative closure. The nonverbal scan of an observer is needed. An observer mode can be elicited even without the nonverbal access provided by hypnosis or drawing if the right brain can be activated. A video clip of an actor portraying the startle, thwarted intention, freeze, etc. of the Instinctual Trauma

Response can be enough to evoke this observer mode (Tinnin & Gantt, 1999).

The therapist can prompt, "Now picture with your mind's eye that little boy you were when he felt trapped and just froze and looked like that." At the same time, an intellectual discussion of the instinctual response can help ground the person in the present. If this discussion while viewing the video can be recorded and replayed, it will promote the development and avowal of the trauma narrative.

### The hypnotic narrative

Ernest Hilgard (1977) experimented with the hypnotic induction of analgesia and discovered that a Hidden Observer could be elicited in those subjects claiming to feel no pain (produced by ischemia of the arm deprived of circulation by the tourniquet effect of an inflated blood pressure cuff). He asked for a report by a part of the subject that did feel the pain and could rate the severity. Some subjects responded from a part of themselves that was aware of the pain and could rate it on a scale of ten during the time the subject had claimed analgesia. These elicited parts were very much alike from subject to subject. The part was normally hidden from the subject's awareness. The part claimed to have always been there. The part was aware of the experimentally induced pain but it denied suffering. Dr. Hilgard designated these parts "Hidden Observers." The Hidden Observers claimed to be onlookers of the person's experiences at all times, whether the subject was hypnotized or not. They played no role in executing action and did not participate in the emotional experience of the subject.

More than 90% of the patients undergoing hypnosis in our clinic were able to liberate a Hidden Observer. Following hypnotic induction by progressive relaxation, the patient visualizes an imaginary scene and executes the imaginary action of stepping out of the body and observing the body from the outside. The therapist refers to the onlooker as the Hidden Observer and points out the capacity for emotional detachment from the patient. The Hidden Observer then temporarily leaves the patient in the imagined scene and goes to observe the traumatic event as it unfolds. The Hidden Observer narrates the event in the third person (referring to the observed self as "he" or "she"), impassively telling the story from beginning to end. The narration is recorded by video camera for the patient's subsequent review in a normal waking state. The session ends after the Hidden Observer returns to the self left in the imagined scene.

- *Case example*

*Fifty-year-old James lays on the recliner with his eyes closed. The therapist speaks. "Now, Hidden Observer, you watched and studied 5-year-old Jimmy going through the tonsillectomy. You saw that he did not die even though he felt he was dying and you watched him being returned to his mother after the recovery room. Now that you can see that he is alright, you can leave this scene and return to the imaginary European village where you find adult James standing on the cobblestone street still gazing at that pocket watch in the window of the shop. Return to your body, look at the watch and describe it." Upon hearing the description and commenting on the special qualities of the watch, the therapist has James leave that scene and return to the office. At the count of five, James opens his eyes and re-orients himself to the present time.*

The hypnotic narrative processing can be completed by reviewing the recorded narrative in the waking state. The patient and the therapist watch the replayed video together. Now the patient no longer has the emotional distance of the Hidden Observer. The patient may only dimly remember much of the narrative, and there is a risk of being triggered into a re-experiencing of the trauma. If this happens, the therapist will stop the replay and help the patient become grounded. The risk is diminished by the ongoing objective study of the Instinctual Trauma Response that the narrative reveals. To promote this objective view, the therapist may periodically stop the video or replay portions of it for closer study.

Usually there is little or no triggering or abreaction with review of the video. This is positive, because abreaction interferes with verbal narrative assimilation. Those elements of the traumatic experience that are not assimilated remain in the nonverbal realm of the mind and are not yet available to long-term narrative memory storage.

A failure to own the narrative is common in patients with dissociative identity disorder. Although the Hidden Observer phenomenon helps the primary personality to learn about the experiences previously kept secret by alter personalities, it may happen in the recursive review that the alter personality reclaims the memory. If portions of the traumatic memory were snatched away during the review, the primary self will be unable to avow the narrative. If this failure is not corrected during the next phase—graphic narration—the entire narrative processing must be repeated. The patient may be able to correct the problem using externalized dialogue (described below) to gain successful negotiation with the alter personality.

### The graphic narrative

The next step in narrative processing is to produce a graphic depiction of the traumatic experience, to which the verbal narrative will be appended. The patient draws a series of pictures that tells the trauma story from beginning to end. Each picture represents a phase of the Instinctual Trauma Response with transition pictures inserted as needed to maintain narrative continuity. This depiction of the nonverbal survival instincts essentially forms the plot of the final narrative. The verbal narrative supplies the script of the story, and the re-presentation made by a therapist promotes avowal of the combined narrative as historical. The graphic narrative is bracketed by a *before* picture and an *after* picture.

Usually there are eight pictures, but sometimes one or more of the instinctual phases was not experienced. This occurs most often in the case of repetitive abuse when the victim lapses into a freeze or altered state of consciousness when triggered by the perpetrator. We ask the patient to identify the body sensations in each picture that might become "body memories" later.

*1. A "before" picture*

*2. The startle*

*3. The fight/flight state*

*4. The freeze state*

*5. The altered state of consciousness*

*6. The state of automatic obedience*

*7. Attempts at self-repair*

*8. The "after" picture to establish endpoint and closure*

In a situation of overwhelming danger, the startle response initiates the cascade of biological reactions that include involuntary posturing, paralysis, obedience, and numbing (Simons, 1996).

In the fight/flight state, there is often a specific "thwarted intention" (usually to take some protective action) or "fixed idea" (such as, "I'm going to die") just before the onset of the freeze state when the victim feels trapped. This suspended urge or notion may later haunt the survivor as an intrusive symptom. The graphic narrative puts the thwarted intention into context. Re-presentation of the graphic narrative will attach words to the nonverbal sensations of the adrenalin rush, the explosive muscle energy, and the heart pounding of the fight/flight state. Thus, the verbal thwarted intention and the nonverbal instinctual state become contextualized.

The freeze state abruptly replaces the fight/flight reaction when the victim is trapped. With an endorphin rush, the body switches into a shutdown state, and the person loses grounding in, and ownership of, the body, which may become immobilized and numb. The bodily numbing and paralysis produces a depersonalization in which a person might feel detached from the body boundaries. The patient commonly depicts this by drawing a small second self, suspended above the body, where the victim watches the event as if it were happening to someone else. The bodily sensations experienced but not consciously registered during this altered state will tend to recur as intrusive body memories and may lead to misdiagnosis as physical ailments (Scaer, 2001; 2005).

There is a self-repair phase in many traumatic experiences that comes after the period of danger but still involves a traumatized mental state. In the aftermath of trauma, the combat veteran and the rape victim each might try to wash off the blood. When this experience is reactivated, they may find themselves compulsively washing repeatedly years later.

When the patient narrates these experiences and links them to the reenactment symptoms that had been thought to be signs of disease, then the symptoms cease. This will only happen after the nonverbal traumatic experience has been converted to history. The patient must fill in all the gaps in the memory and own the event as personal history.

The patient might begin a graphic narrative of an unremembered trauma by drawing a dream image or a flashback image or even a scribble and then expanding it with what "must have come next." The patient allows images to emerge with the faith that "the hand remembers though the mind forgets." One may overcome a block to progressing by doing a map picture, depicting a bird's eye view, or drawing a zoom picture enlarging an element of a picture. Drawing one's body from the perspective of the Hidden Observer helps the patient stay grounded.

The patient can similarly gain access to preverbal images that were laid down in memory during infancy, before language and before verbal coding of memory developed. The intrusive symptoms arising from preverbal traumatic memories usually reenact bodily experience in symptoms such as being unable to breathe (originating, for example, in infantile apnea or smothering or surgical anesthesia), diffuse pain with focal points in pelvis, genitals, or rectum (from infantile sexual abuse by probing or penetration, enemas, painful medical procedures, etc.), or other bodily distress. The patient might construct the nonverbal narrative by first depicting the sensation and then allowing spontaneous drawing to elaborate the body memory into a picture narrative. These body memories cease as soon as the trauma is narrated and verbally avowed.

- *Re-presentation of graphic narratives*

When the nonverbal traumatic experience has been verbally coded and assimilated, the patient comes to own the narrative as personal history. Completing the drawing of the narrative does not automatically accomplish this avowal. The patient may still see the event as happening to someone else or may still be unable to believe that the trauma could happen.

The patient can most easily affirm and own the narrative if it is "re-presented." Simply displaying the pictures in narrative sequence at a distance beyond arm's reach begins the re-presentation. The patient beholds the picture story "out there" as an external depiction of a past event and begins to own the event, usually in gradual increments. The therapist assists the patient's verbal assimilation by "reading" the pictures (Figure 4) and dramatizing the story in words. The therapist merges the wordless experiences of each instinctual state into the verbal narrative.

- ### *Review re-presentation*

Because the avowal may occur in increments, it is helpful for the patient to review the re-presentation. This is easily accomplished if the re-presentation by the therapist is video recorded for the patient's homework reviews. If the video equipment is not available at home, it is wise to repeat the re-presentation by the therapist at least once in a later session.

- ### *Avowal of narrative*

The patient with DID may approach the narrative construction somewhat differently. The graphic narrative may be drawn by one or more alter personalities contributing their knowledge of portions of the experience in which they were involved. The process of re-presentation and avowal is just the same as with the other patients. The primary personality (the host personality or main personality) participates in the review and is responsible for the avowal, owning the body and owning the event even though alter personalities had owned the experiences before. It may take longer for the dissociative patient to accomplish full avowal because of the ownership of portions of the memory by alter personalities, but the externalized narrative stands as impressive evidence for the primary personality to use. Alter person-alities may resist the assimilation of their traumatic memories into the externalized narrative because they sense that this might lead to their own assimilation. In fact, if the graphic narrative endows closure to the trauma, the alter personality is liberated from that previously dissociated experience that was suspended in time. This removes the block to change, and it becomes possible for the alter personality to relate to the present and to negotiate change with the patient. Later, we will see how this is done using the externalized dialogue.

- ### *Outcome of graphic narrative processing*

If the patient successfully completes the graphic narrative and avows it as personal history, then any intrusive symptoms that were due to this trauma should cease completely. A partial effect should occur within days and a full effect within weeks. If this

# RE-PRESENTATION OF GRAPHIC NARRATIVE

*Figure 4*

does not happen, either the processing was incomplete or the symptoms relate, at least partially, to another trauma.

The first step is to repeat the narrative processing. Usually this second narration is more detailed and complete and makes it possible to fill in gaps that were not detected during the first. When this does not relieve the intrusive symptoms, the cause might be that the symptoms arise from earlier traumas. The patient may have to search for unremembered traumas, such as preverbal ones or overlooked traumas due to medical or surgical procedures, for example. Sometimes recurrent nightmares may persist even after the trauma that originally caused the nightmare is resolved. The patient can stop this form of recurrent nightmare by drawing a narrative closure to it. The artist devises an ending to the dream and draws a graphic narrative of it. The therapist re-presents the dream narrative. The devised ending need not be a happy conclusion. It needs only to bring closure to the narrative.

If all else fails and the intrusive symptoms persist, the trauma processing can go on to the next phase of treatment and return to the graphic narrative later.

The response of arousal symptoms usually follows that of intrusive symptoms with only a slight delay of perhaps several days. It is a different story for the numbing or avoidant symptoms. There is usually some improvement in the emotional numbing and attachment problems after successful processing, but a full response usually must await resolution of the person's victim mythology and dissociative symptoms.

### Repair of traumatic dissociation

The Instinctual Trauma Response leaves in its wake at least four dissociated elements: memory fragments, fixed ideas, fixed states, and traumatized selves. Individuals with complex post-traumatic disorder or dissociative disorder may harbor a variety of interacting dissociated parts generated by repeated traumatic experiences.

- *Memory shrapnel*

Fragmented perceptions of the traumatic experience can remain embedded deep in nonverbal memory as memory shrapnel. This metaphor appeals to combat veterans in particular. This unidentified element sometimes blocks narrative closure even when the Instinctual Trauma Response has been narrated. Such a memory fragment usually emerges as a component of a flashback image but it may escape notice when paired with some other overwhelming part.

- *Case example*

*A 39-year-old tow truck driver was called to tow a stolen automobile that was being examined by a police officer. The tow truck arrived as the officer was beginning his inspection of the car. They did not suspect that it might be booby-trapped, but it was. An explosive charge was connected to the inner dome light, to be detonated when current flowed to the light.*

*The tow truck driver stood behind the car waiting for the order to attach the towing apparatus. The officer was at the passenger door; when he opened the door, the car blew up. The tow truck driver was lifted and hurled backward by the blast. Both men were badly wounded but they survived.*

*It was three months later when the tow truck driver sought help for his continuing state of shock and fear with severe flashbacks and dreams of the trauma. He worked diligently to construct a graphic narrative of the traumatic experience but failed to gain relief of his flashbacks until he reworked the drawings to include a critical missing element. When he slowed down the image of his body hurtling backwards through the air, he pictured a large shard of glass slicing toward his face and remembered his sense of doom and certainty of death. Somehow, the shard did not slice through his face. He drew the scene depicting the shard as barely missing his head. The narrative was finally complete, and his symptoms yielded quickly to the final processing of the trauma.*

- ### *Fixed ideas*

A second dissociated element is an idea that remains fixed with all of its initial emotional impact such as, "I am dying," or "My body is dead." Such fixed ideas haunt the dreams of survivors and are sometimes the origin of bizarre symptoms such as perceptions that one's body is alien or unrecognizable in the mirror or a feeling of being dead.

- ### *Fixed states*

We described fixed states above as the unshakable influence of one or another phase of the Instinctual Trauma Response, that continues under the surface as if the traumatic experience never finished. It is usually organized as a latent mental system dedicated to protection of the self as known at the time of the trauma. A tragic example is the *sitting duck syndrome* described by Richard Kluft (1990). The victim of repeated childhood sexual abuse left with a fixed state of automatic obedience may be unable to say "no" to a sexual predator.

- *Traumatized selves*

A major dissociated element created by trauma is a frozen replica of the victim at the onset or other point during the experience. These parts may have particular burdens such as self-appointed carriers of pain or keepers of secrets.

## Externalized dialogue

The individual is usually not aware of the presence of dissociated memory fragments, fixed ideas, or fixed states even though these elements may powerfully affect one's actions and feelings. The presence of dissociated selves more often gains notice as inner voices or alter personalities. When one does realize the presence of a dissociated self, it becomes possible to have an inner verbal dialogue with that self. Inner dialogues can lead to negotiation and resolution of differences, which can diminish the differentiation between inner and outer person and therefore weaken dissociation. In practice, people find it difficult to do that negotiation and resolution by inner dialogue alone. It is hard to stick to the basic verbal structure of thesis, antithesis, and synthesis necessary for negotiation and problem solving. An inner dialogue is less civil than spoken dialogue in which the participants respectfully take turns and avoid interrupting each other. The externalized dialogue provides access to—and a coherent means of communication with—dissociated elements. The basic rules for externalized dialogue are to take turns and not interrupt.

- *Techniques for the externalized dialogue*

In the externalized dialogue, a person simply takes turns speaking from one and then the other position or point of view. The exchange can be merely role-playing. Frequently it is surprisingly authentic for the person when the messages are unexpected and carry unremembered facts and feelings. Different forms of external communication with oneself have been used therapeutically. Gestalt therapists have used the empty chair method (Perls, 1969). Others have used a conference room set-up that allows a person to speak out for different inner parts (Fraser, 1991). We use several approaches to promote the turn-taking and to provide a recording or written version for later review. Our preference is the video dialogue, but some patients prefer other methods such as audio recording, writing, or typing.

- *Video dialogue*

We learned about the special property of the recorded video image to diminish a person's distortion of one's own body image from the work of Richard Seimi at West Virginia University. He studied the distortion of body image in patients with anorexia nervosa. He was able to measure the degree of distortion by manipulating the TV image with a dial that could make the person appear thinner or fatter (Szymanski & Seime, 1997). The patients perceived their video image more accurately than they did their mirror image. They were able to designate the point at which the image they changed with the dial matched their perceived mirror image.

We found a similar phenomenon when we showed our patients with DID the video recording of their alter personalities. The brunette patient was surprised to see dark hair on her presumed blonde alter. The power of the video to undercut distortion is not absolute and varies from person to person but it helps a great deal to establish the fact of a single body for all of the alters. It also provides a means by which the individual can overcome the dissociative barrier between multiple personalities. A video dialogue makes it possible for the patient to negotiate with the alter personalities and keep a record of it.

The necessary equipment is a video camera and television monitor or other means of playback. The therapist and patient sit side-by-side, which averts the patient feeling scrutinized while speaking and reserves it for joint scrutiny when viewing the play-backs. The objective is for the patient to develop a spoken dialogue with a part of the self, such as an inner personality, voice, or ego state.

Usually the first move is for the patient to look into the eye of the camera and invite the other participant (inner child, voice, etc.) to take turns talking. The invitation may be brief or it can be an extended appeal for communication. When the invitation is completed, the therapist prepares the speaker to now become the listener. By saying something such as "Now empty your mind to allow that inner self to watch and listen carefully." After the re-play, the therapist sets up the video camera to record the patient speaking for the other participant. Setting a different focal distance (e.g., less "zoom") helps to differentiate the speakers when the video recording is replayed and studied uninterrupted later.

The therapist may simply say, "Now look into the eye of the camera and speak for…" (e.g. "the child"). On the other hand, the therapist might encourage a dissociated response by saying, "Close your eyes while I count to seven, and at the count of seven the child will open your eyes and take his turn." In later exchanges, the therapist can simply announce the speaker, for example, "Little Jane talks to adult Jane."

When the response to the invitation is finished, the therapist prepares the playback and, again sitting side-by-side, patient and therapist watch the recorded message. The therapist may now act as a coach to the primary patient with encouragement or advice about approaching negotiation or making a deal. We believe that the best practice is to limit the therapist's coaching or counseling to the primary patient and to preserve the patient's own responsibility for leadership in relating to the other participants.

Back and forth, the dialogue goes, and there is often a considerable contention between the participants. The previously silent inner part now has a voice and can speak out in anger and bitterness for having been suppressed by the patient. The patient may have to deal with mistrust and even serious antipathy. It is not unusual in cases of early childhood sexual abuse for the adult patient to feel a strong antipathy toward the inner child. These issues and the polarization between the participants are the targets for negotiation. When compromises are reached or agreements are made the participants become less differentiated from each other and dissociation wanes.

The usual goal of the externalized dialogue is for the dissociated part to enter into the present life of the patient. The patient finds ways to assure safety and to welcome that part into this world.

- ### *Hemifield goggles*

Our theoretical assumption about the brain dynamics of traumatic memories is that these memories were acquired during a period of diminished cerebral dominance and that they are stored in the nonverbal brain without the benefit of verbal narrative organization. If this is so, then most traumatized people will carry these dissociated memories in the nondominant brain hemisphere. Even if the cerebral storage of memory were not segregated by anatomical region, the access to dissociated memory would be via nonverbal routes and through the nonverbal hemisphere.

66

In the process of repairing dissociation by externalized dialogue, it is useful to selectively activate the nonverbal hemisphere. A unique means of accomplishing this was offered by Fredric Schiffer of Harvard University. He devised a means of altering a person's visual field so that one or the other hemisphere is selectively activated (Schiffer, 1998). He altered safety goggles to allow vision out of one visual field only. He found that half of his patients had the response of feeling their symptoms intensify with the open visual field on one side and diminish with it on the other. About half of those who responded showed a dramatic response.

We copied his device but altered the taping somewhat so that both eyes can see through the selected right or left visual field (Figure 5). With the left visual field open—that is, each lens of the safety goggles have the right half masked by tape—the light entering the eyes from the left stimulates the right hemisphere. The patient can switch from the left hemifield goggles to the right ones easily to do a video dialogue with selective hemispheric activation for each participant.

Most adult patients manage a productive video dialogue without using the goggles, but a few find they can gain more differentiation between the participants by using the goggles. The goggles are particularly helpful when using the video dialogue for the problem of victim mythology. They bring out the pessimistic versus optimistic views more selectively.

We have not found a predictable response to the different goggles. Some people report no difference between them. Others feel distinctly uncomfortable and cannot wait to take off the disturbing pair. One woman had complained that for years she had been plagued by an intrusive visual symptom of a tiny "video screen" in the corner of her right eye. This screen displayed a continuous movie of "everything bad" that she had ever experienced. She had an immediate relief when she found which pair of goggles stopped the image. Some six years later she reported that she sometimes had a recurrence of the "movie" but that she could turn it off with a bit of mental effort.

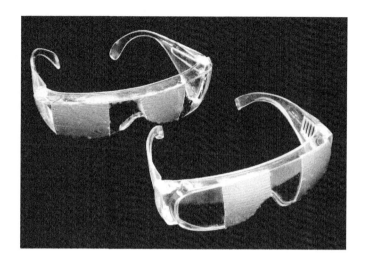

*Figure 5*

- ***Masks***

Some trauma patients cannot stand to see themselves on the video monitor. They may be similarly repelled by their image in the mirror or in photographs. This post-traumatic body dysmorphia seems to correlate with the degree of victim mythology and expresses the individual's sense of being damaged or flawed by the trauma. Some of these patients will absolutely refuse video dialogue. Others will agree to participate using masks. We constructed papier-mâché masks attached to a stick for holding them in front of the face (Figure 6). The person speaks from behind the mask using a different mask for each participant.

- ***Other techniques for externalized dialogue***

One can sculpt in clay an inner dissociated part such as the traumatized child and talk to—and for—the sculpture in a video dialogue. When the person speaks for the child, the camera zooms in on the sculpture. In the replay, the patient sees the sculpture while listening to the message. After the patient responds in turn and the response is replayed, the patient may hold the sculpture while listening on behalf of the inner child.

Children and young adolescents generally do not take to the standard video dialogue. They can participate well if the participants are represented as clay sculptures, puppets, or stuffed animals. Adolescents like to script a dialogue using toys as actors in a "play." Younger children can respond to a video dialogue in which someone else plays the participants.

- *Case example*

    *Thirteen-year-old Tony's life seemed to fall apart after he had oral surgery for impacted wisdom teeth. There was no obvious complication at the time of surgery. The anesthesia was the usual local injection supplemented with nitrous*

## MASKS FOR VIDEO DIALOGUE

*Figure 6*

*oxide gas inhaled through a nose mask. The surgeon did not notice any sign of undue distress, and Tony's post-operative course was not unusual. However, at home and at school Tony was not the same. He was tense and nervous and had nightmares. He could not concentrate well, and his schoolwork deteriorated. He showed spells of immobility and staring, and observers feared that he was having absence seizures. Extensive neurological evaluations could not explain the spells or provide any diagnosis. A variety of medical consultants and nonmedical healers were consulted. Trials of medications and other remedies failed to help.*

*Finally, a child psychiatrist suggested that Tony could be suffering from a post-traumatic syndrome due to an unidentified trauma. Arrangements were made for the parents to drive Tony to West Virginia for treatment at the trauma center. Tony revealed under hypnosis that he had experienced the Instinctual Trauma Response during the oral surgery. He panicked, went into a freeze state, and believed he felt himself die and leave his body. He completed the hypnotic narrative processing of the experience. After awakening and reviewing the videotape, he remembered it all clearly. He completed a graphic narrative without difficulty but he could not bring himself to do a video dialogue.*

*His parents did the video dialogue for him. His father spoke for Tony in the surgery having a near-death experience, and his mother spoke for the present Tony needing to have his old self back. They negotiated a reunion between "Old Self" and "New Self" to be consummated during the upcoming visit to his grandparents' house. When the family reviewed the videotaped dialogue, Tony was ecstatic. Tony had spent only a day and a half in the outpatient evaluation and treatment, and from that day on, he was back to his old self and had no return of symptoms.*

- *Written Dialogue*

An externalized dialogue in writing is portable and convenient. Some people can write legibly with either hand. Left-hand writing is an excellent conduit for expression by a dissociated part and particularly so for child parts. In the dialogue, right and left hands take turns.

It is not absolutely necessary for the written dialogue to involve both hands. It can be effective using the dominant hand only. The dialogue can be typed. Some individuals exchange e-mails or text messages between the dialogue participants. Some patients do their homework dialogues by audiotape recording. Any medium will serve for externalized dialogues as long as it permits turn taking and review of the messages.

## Phase 3: Parts work and repair of victim mythology

### Working with parts

Working with latent mental systems has become a major part of our treatment program. It arose naturally from the original use of externalized dialogues to recruit the frozen traumatized self into the present life of the patient. We used the externalized dialogue increasingly for the inner parts of patients that spoke to them in the form of auditory hallucinations and then for the parts that urged suicide or self-harming, impulsive, or addictive behavior. It is important to remember that inner parts may communicate with the person by extreme urge or strong feeling as well as by voice. From the very beginning, the trauma therapist's response was to coach the patient to deal with the part by persuasion or negotiation. The success of this response supported a central principle in the work with dissociative patients. That is, the therapist does not enter a relationship with a dissociated part (including ego states, subpersonalities, and alter personalities) but instead promotes the patient's leadership and communication with the parts.

Our approach is influenced by Schwartz's Internal Family Systems (IFS) model (Goulding & Schwartz, 2002), the ego state model of Watkins and Watkins (1997) and parts psychology as described by Jay Noricks (Noricks, 2011). These writers' general conception of parts is similar to ours, but our view of the origin and development of latent mental systems is different. The Instinctual Trauma

Response model assumes dissociated parts to arise from adverse events that are serious enough to interrupt the normal cerebral dominance of the verbal mind.

If the event is sufficiently traumatic to elicit an individual's survival instincts then the instinctual state of mind may remain a dissociated part of the person, frozen in time, largely inaccessible to the flow of verbal consciousness. If the person later manages to process the experience and gain verbal narrative closure to it, then the dissociated part will no longer be locked into the past. However, that part may have developed a mind of its own and may reject the natural move to participate as part of the person's present life. At this point, dialogues between self and part afford opportunity to recruit the part into the person's present life.

Once dissociated parts are formed, they are relatively permanent. They may or may not have awareness of the greater self or of other parts. If they are aware of others, they may have roles or carry burdens related to the others and to the trauma. The effect of their roles or burdens (for example, of secrecy, defense, attachment, entitlement, or guilt and shame) may be felt faintly or overwhelmingly by the person. The therapist's knowledge about parts can help guide the patient to successful negotiation with parts.

Entry into parts work might begin with the first dialogue in the first trauma processing. For example, following the graphic narrative processing of a preverbal trauma when the patient seeks to access the inner baby part for an externalized dialogue but encounters a block due to a sense of alarm, an IFS technique can be applied. The therapist instructs the person to address the sense of alarm as a part and ask it to step back temporarily while the person talks with the baby. When the patient is able to do this and completes the externalized dialogue, parts work has begun. At the opportune time, the alarmed part can be identified, mapped, and unburdened.

Once the patient is able to differentiate parts (latent mental systems) from the greater self (dominant mental system), it becomes possible to converse, negotiate, unburden, and find solutions acceptable to the parts and the self. The therapist encourages the patient to emphasize that no one is going to kill or get rid of any part. If a part does not agree to participate, the patient can try for agreement to at least not hinder or sabotage therapy.

## Current concepts of dissociation

The structural theory of dissociation jointly developed by scholars in the Netherlands and the United States (Van der Hart, et al., 2006) has been helpful to our understanding of latent mental systems. We incorporated aspects of their theory into our dual-brain model. Our concept begins with the demonstrated fact that the two cerebral hemispheres of the infant do not communicate with each other until after three years of age when the connecting corpus callosum first begins to transmit information between the two hemispheres (Salamy, 1978). The following illustration (Figure 7) refers to this as preverbal dissociation:

### PREVERBAL DISSOCIATION

*Immature corpus callosum*

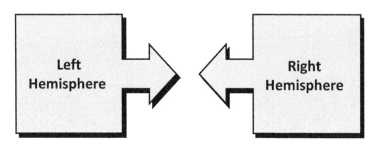

*Figure 7*

When the child reaches three years of age, or shortly thereafter, the corpus callosum matures sufficiently for transmission of information from one to the other hemisphere (Figure 8). At this point, there is a competition between the left hemisphere and the right hemisphere for dominance. In normal development, the outcome of this competition decides where the "I" of the person will reside.

## AGE 3 – RIGHT & LEFT BRAIN COMMUNICATION

*Corpus callosum begins transmission and competition for dominance ensues*

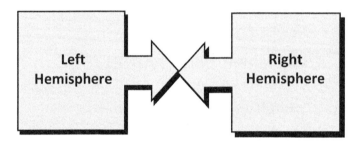

*Figure 8*

The left hemisphere wins 70% of the time (Annett, 1998) and when it does it will contain the verbal mind and will rule over the nonverbal mind by exercising cerebral dominance. When the child attains spoken language and verbal thinking, the dominant verbal mind will claim ownership of the whole self and deny the actual duality of mind. However, the right brain contains memory of preverbal times and increasingly operates the central management of the body's interior, including the immune system, the endocrine system, and the digestive system. The verbal mind dismisses all of that as "it" while it communicates with the world as "I" (Figure 9). If there is no adverse event serious enough to elicit the instinctual survival patterns of the trauma response, the left brain will continue to dominate and the right brain to submit. Callosal traffic is active although under the direction of the left brain. (For a comparison of the two brains, see McManus, 2002; Siegel, 2010; Zaidel & Iacoboni, 2003.)

# CEREBRAL DOMINANCE

*Illusion of Mental Unity, Verbal Brain = "I"*

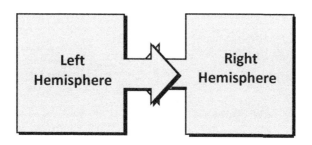

*Figure 9*

If a traumatic event elicits the Instinctual Trauma Response, which will interrupt cerebral dominance and the verbal coding of memory, the result will have the same effect as would a physical interruption of the corpus callosum (Figure 10).

The traumatized person may recover from the Instinctual Trauma Response, but the brain is now changed. The traumatic experience left its imprint on the nonverbal mind when the verbal mind relinquished dominance. Although the person may retain some verbal memory of the experience, the nonverbal memory is not in narrative form and is deprived of the temporal ordering of verbal memory. The right hemisphere holds the perceptions and sensations frozen in time, in perpetual present tense. It is as if the left hemisphere disavows the reaction to the trauma and ignores the pain of the right. Van der Hart, et al. (2006) designate this as "primary dissociation" (Figure 11).

# TRAUMATIC EVENT

## Cerebral Dominance Interrupted

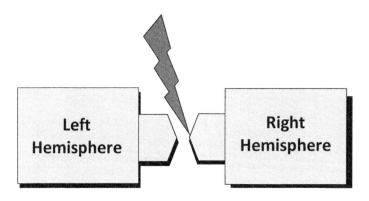

Trauma Response = Right Hemisphere Survival
Strategies

*Figure 10*

The emotional self is relatively unavailable to the verbal mind, which results in a condition termed *alexithymia* (Taylor & Taylor, 1997) People in this state may find verbal consciousness retracted. From time to time, they may lose control and lapse into a nonverbal traumatized state. In their most stable verbal state, they will still be without the normal access to their emotional selves.

More severe or prolonged trauma can lead to secondary dissociation (Figure 12) according to Van der Hart, et al. (2006). The nonverbal personality becomes compartmentalized. Each trauma leaves one or more traumatized selves frozen in time. The repeated instinctual trauma reactions result in fixed survival patterns that may develop as parts exercise their survival skills with determined intention and direction. Secondary dissociation makes for the clinical syndrome we term dissociative disorder not otherwise specified (DDNOS).

# PRIMARY DISSOCIATION

*Weakened Callosal Transmission*

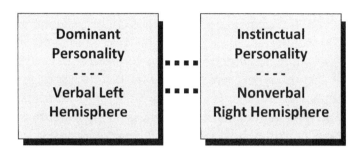

*Figure 11*

## SECONDARY DISSOCIATION
*Instinctual Personality*
*Compartmentalized*

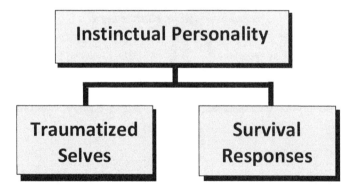

*Figure 12*

The parts that remain as traumatized selves (Figure 13) usually experience themselves as the age when the trauma occurred, but this is not always so and they may age as the person does. These parts are usually locked into the trauma of their origin and often have little awareness of the current experiences of the person. When the person processes the traumatic memory and gains closure, the part remains. The part is no longer locked in the traumatic experience and would be free to participate, along with other parts, in the present, but it may be disdainful or hostile to the greater self or it may be burdened by some protective duty to the old self. The preverbal parts are often the most active through their needy attachment cries. They are also the most removed from the person's awareness, although their neediness and their more primitive urges may blend with the person's consciousness.

**TRAUMATIZED SELVES**

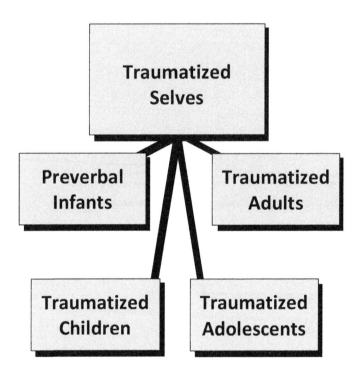

*Figure 13*

# SURVIVAL RESPONSE PARTS

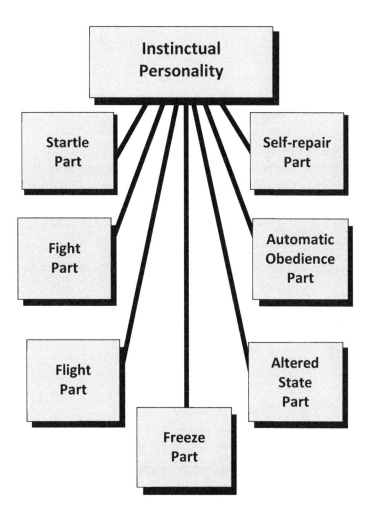

*Figure 14*

The survival responses to a trauma may persist as latent mental systems dedicated to protective survival roles (Figure 14). They may be potent influences in the person's fight or flight reactions to everyday events or in avoidant behaviors or fearful states. When a patient deals with these inner parts by means of externalized dialogue and negotiation, it can bring a great emotional and behavioral relief.

The latent mental systems as survival response parts tend to have certain characteristics. First, they are generally gullible and quite responsive to re-framing of their roles and duties. Their emotional armor quickly melts in the warmth of the self's acceptance. However, these parts can be narrow-minded and irrationally fierce in their extreme and sometimes perverted attempts to protect such as urging suicide or self-mutilation. They often present themselves as if in a Wizard-of-Oz drama as little kids hiding behind a frightening mask. They may also hide duplicates of themselves. Parts may have parts.

Extreme repetitive traumas may give rise to tertiary dissociation (Figure 15), the hallmark of DID. In this case, the real-world

## TERTIARY DISSOCIATION

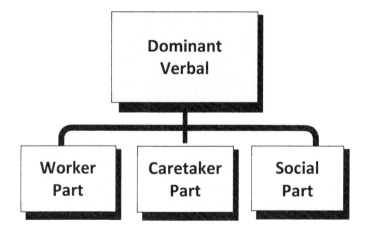

*Figure 15*

coping roles of the overwhelmed verbal personality differentiate from that personality into independent actors. These parts are usually verbal and are usually older than elementary school age.

Dissociated parts can take any form, animate or inanimate, person or animal. Whatever their shape or characteristics, they can be communicated with and deals can be struck. The more common parts are those described so far. One of the most problematic of parts is the internalized perpetrator who commonly resists negotiation (Figure 16).

Schwartz describes the internal psychological milieu of the parts as "Internal Family Systems" (Goulding & Schwartz, 2002) that emphasizes interactions between the parts. Keep in mind that while some traumatized self-parts are too locked in the past trauma as their present world, others may actively respond to what goes on in the outside world. The response of one part may provoke reactions by others (Figure 17).

### Objectives of parts work

There is controversy in the field of dissociative disorders about the desirable endpoint of therapy. Early in the twentieth century, it was assumed that cure required a fusion of parts into a unitary mind free of dissociation. The idea that the normal mind is unitary has gradually given way to the conception of a normal dissociative or modular mind with multiple streams of thought, but consensus has not been reached.

We observe that the follow-up testing normalizes to our criteria of recovery when the patient has succeeded in getting all the parts onto "the team." When full communication with all the parts through externalized dialogue has been achieved and there is a democratic cooperation in the team, the testing registers normal, which we consider full recovery. Our goal is for a cooperative integration of parts rather than a merging of the parts into one.

### Mapping of parts

Art therapy provides one of the basic concepts of our trauma therapy, which is to externalize the inner image, thought, or dialogue. This makes it possible for the patient to work with important and difficult mental contents with the eye of an observing ego. This is a key to success in providing practical brief

## TYPES OF DISSOCIATED PARTS

- **Traumatized self states**
- **Instinctual survival response parts**
- **Hypervigilant protector parts**
- **Managerial parts**
- **Perpetrator parts**

*Figure 16*

## EXAMPLE OF THE DYNAMICS OF PARTS

- **Child part seeking attachment clings to the therapist**
- **Flight/fight protector creates distance, sabotages therapy, threatens suicide to defend against danger of attachment**
- **Child part increases attachment cry**
- **Hypervigilant protectors become more extreme**

  *And 'round and 'round the cycle goes!*

*Figure 17*

therapy without the complication of abreaction. The patient is empowered by the objective grasp afforded by putting the elements of concern "out there" on the paper or in clay.

That empowerment is useful when an individual must work with inner parts. The empowerment begins with externalizing a dialogue with a part and it increases when that part is mapped "out there" in a manner that shows the relation of one part to other parts and to the greater self. This can be accomplished with diagrams showing the placement of parts with some means of designating their ages, sex, origin, roles, and burdens. The mapping is enhanced if the parts are represented on index cards or Post-It notes and can be attached to a base and moved as needed (Figure 18). Cork boards, large pieces of heavy art paper, or a white board can be used as the base. Individual bases that can be put away between sessions are preferred but if that is not feasible, photographs or Xerox copies will be sufficient.

## MAPPING

*Figure 18*

## Treatment of victim mythology

The first and so-called "primary" dissociation caused by trauma is part of a diminished communication between the left and right brain hemispheres so that the conscious verbal self is less attuned to the subconscious nonverbal self. During the period of the Instinctual Trauma Response, the verbal conscious mind has relinquished cerebral dominance, leaving the nonverbal self bereft of leadership and orientation in time. After the trauma, when verbal dominance is resumed, the traumatic perceptions and emotions remain as memories without narrative organization or verbal coding. The traumatic interruption of communication between the hemispheres does not fully recover with the resumption of cerebral dominance. It is *as if* the function of the corpus callosum, which sends nerve impulses from one hemisphere to the other, is diminished. The usual integration between the emotional right brain and the logical left brain is impaired.

At this point, the individual has changed. The presenting personality is more constricted in terms of emotional attunement to self and others. The clinical term for this is "alexithymia" (Sifneos, 1988), literally meaning a loss of words for feelings. Closer examination reveals an active avoidance of awareness of the emotional memory of the right brain. Pierre Janet termed this "trauma phobia" and explained it as the resistance of the patient to thinking and feeling about the trauma. The loss of attunement deprives the nonverbal mind of the support and guidance of the conscious mind, and the nonverbal mind becomes overcome by the traumatic experiences that will not recede into the past. The nonverbal mind becomes vulnerable to current reminders that trigger the seemingly unfinished traumatic experience.

The trauma victim's pessimistic take on life is fueled by the unending traumatic stress experienced by the subconscious traumatized mind. The assumptive world of that mind is one in which one's best hope is simply to survive, and the best guide to living is to keep one's guard up. This victim mythology may suffuse the otherwise logical experience of the left brain. As much as the person may rise above victim mythology by immersion in work or tasks of everyday life, the price that is paid can be measured by the severity of alexithymia as measured by the Toronto Alexithymia Scale (Bagby, Parker, & Taylor, 1994). In the best of times and more often during the day the person's left brain is dominant and the person may appear relatively normal. In the darkness of night and in bad times the person's right brain gains ascendancy and victim mythology prevails.

Full recovery from trauma requires a restoration of normal left brain-right brain connection and, to some extent, a relinquishing of the left brain's illusion of mental unity. First, trauma phobia must be overcome. The narrative processing of the traumatic experiences is the most effective way to accomplish this. Traumatic memory becomes avowed by the person and transformed to acknowledged personal history. Re-experiencing of the trauma then is no longer to be feared.

Alexithymia can be reversed by open dialogue between the right and left brains. The left brain comes to accept a new partnership with the right. There is a relaxation of the left-brain dominance, a lessening of right brain submission, and a new acceptance of mental duality in place of strict mental unity.

Our clinical experience shows that dialogue around three particular issues promotes the reversal of victim mythology: (1) relinquishing pursuit of the childhood illusion of invulnerability; (2) resolution of shame and guilt; and (3) relinquishing of the feeling of entitlement. Treatment of victim mythology can be approached by dialogue with the parts that carry the survival burden of safety, the emotional burden of shame and guilt, and the relational burden of entitlement.

### The burden of safety

Those parts arising from trauma during the pre-school years experience the most extreme responsibility for safety. They demand that the self achieve absolute invulnerability to bring them a feeling of safety. One woman in her forties finally achieved a modicum of safety by equipping her apartment with locks, alarms, and blinds, but this was at the cost of a social life and her job. Still, that inner voice was not satisfied.

The all-or-none, black-and-white thinking of the parts most rooted in the survival instincts is responsible for much of the extreme aspect of intrusions by parts. This mode of thinking makes the trauma patient's fearfulness quite resistant to conventional therapy.

However, when the self of the patient addresses the part as a parent addresses a child, the resistance is more manageable. Below is an example of addressing a four-year-old part in an externalized dialogue.

> *"Honey, you are a part of me, a precious part of me, and I am now a grown-up that can take care of you and always keep you safe. Thank you for taking care of us when I was four years old too. Now, finally, I can take care of you and you can feel safe like you always wanted me to feel. Now you can feel safe and not only that but you can have fun with me and with the things we do. Next week we will go see the animals at the zoo."*

- ### *Guilt and shame*

Much of the guilt felt by trauma patients is associated with an attempt to rework the trauma. The underlying assumption is that the traumatic experiences are unfinished and continue in the present. There is a continuing guilt for the failure to alter the outcome. "If I had only fought back he wouldn't have abused me." The patient's guilt often resolves as narrative processing of the traumatic memories renders them historical and finished. When guilt is not resolved, the patient can identify the part still experiencing it as unfinished and can help that part bring closure to the memory.

Shame is usually related to the experience of absolute helplessness that one experiences when the fight/flight instinct is thwarted and one feels defeated. Many patients with prominent shame experienced the freeze state as death and carry the sense of a part of them being dead. Lacking the understanding of their responses as instinctual, they attribute their feeling of shame to their passivity in the trauma. The patient can deal with shamed parts by acknowledging and normalizing the helplessness and by affirming that they did not die.

- ### *Entitlement*

It is not surprising that a person wounded by others would feel entitled to apology and reparation. Reparation for trauma is usually not a realistic possibility, and an unrelenting demand that it be made right can be an obstacle to recovery. The patient may consciously or unconsciously expect the therapist to make it right. This expectation may be generalized to all others. The patient may feel entitled to rescue and relate to others as potential rescuers. The desired rescue and reparation will not be forthcoming, and the patient may feel doomed.

It is much easier to face the issue of entitlement if the patient identifies the parts most concerned with it and helps them to redirect their efforts to more realistic helpful goals.

### Victim mythology in a larger context

The pessimistic assumptive world of victim mythology is not limited to trauma patients. Anyone feeling defeated and untrusting, dealing with extremes of hurt and anger, or oppressed by strong impulses to commit suicide may be experiencing intrusive influences of dissociated parts of themselves. They, too, may benefit from externalized dialogue with those parts. Therapists struggling with these clinical problems might profit by guiding their patients to the self-help of externalized dialogue with their latent mental systems.

## Management of complications in treatment

### Acute trance state

Before the patient achieves closure of the trauma narrative, the emerging images may trigger a dissociative trance. It might be a reenactment of the Instinctual Trauma Response or a reflexive defense against the aroused anxiety. The patient lapses into a trance state, out of contact with the surroundings, and the situation may require immediate intervention. These states may take the form of an out-of-body experience, a catatonic state or frozen reaction, or simply a dazed state. They all share the same loss of cerebral dominance with weak grounding in the context of present time, space, and body. We contend that it is a state of automatic obedience awaiting commands that provide context and direction such as that normally provided by waking consciousness, or in hypnosis, by the hypnotist. It has the basic properties of a hypnotic trance no matter what form it takes. This is not to say that dissociation and hypnosis are the same. Dell (2009) gives an excellent review of that controversy. However, these properties make it possible to approach the trance state as a hypnotic state without a hypnotist.

The therapist can do what a hypnotist does: gain rapport, take control, and issue commands. To gain rapport, the therapist can appropriate some on-going behavior by describing it, such as, "You are breathing in and out, in and out." The therapist takes control by changing the description to conduct the behavior, such as, "You will breathe in and out, in and out." The therapist can then terminate the trance by commanding, for example, "At the count of five you will be back in this room in this present time: one and two and three and four and five."

- *Grounding*

The trance state is liable to recur if the person's grounding in present reality is not strengthened. The goal is to focus conscious attention outward and promote active engagement with the present surroundings. For example, the therapist can do the following: have the patient talk out loud to engage the verbal mind and provide context through language; prescribe goal-directed activity and involve others; or suggest measures to increase contact with the here-and-now and help the person avoid mental rumination, blank staring, meditative states, or day-dreaming. The grounding process should be discussed long before it is needed.

In terms of the Instinctual Trauma Response model, grounding refers to the measures taken to restore verbal cerebral dominance. The effect is to bring the person back to the present time and space, securely reinstalled within the physical body, with a sense of unitary identity, a sense of will, and a capacity for reality monitoring and for verbal communication.

Grounding techniques can use any of the senses or mental operations (such as doing long division or naming items that start with a particular letter.

> **Visual.** Tell the person to "look above eye level and name three things [wait for a response], look at eye level and name three things [wait for a response], look below eye level and name three things [wait for a response]." Keep asking the same things in the same order if the person does not respond quickly.
>
> **Kinesthetic.** "Put your feet on the floor and put your hands on your knees, press down on your knees, feel how the

floor supports your feet, put the small of your back against the back of the chair, feel how the chair supports you." Tell the person to change positions: if sitting, stand up; if standing, sit down. Walk the person around the hall or outside.

**Auditory.** "Listen to the sound of my voice as I bring you back to the here-and-now. You are here in [state the place] and it is [state the date, describe the surroundings and the weather]. At the count of five you will be able to open your eyes and be fully aware and awake."

**Tactile.** Rub a grounding stone, a piece of textured material, or a stuffed animal; put a piece of ice on the inside of the wrist or elbow. Don't touch the person without first saying what you are going to do and see if you can get a nod of the head to do so.

**Olfactory.** Use a pleasant smell such as lavender, cinnamon, or chamomile tea. Put a cotton ball soaked in favorite cologne in a small plastic bag and keep it in a shirt pocket.

Use simple, direct language and a firm reassuring tone of voice. Keep in mind that a person who is dissociating may still hear you (but your voice may sound far away, as if you are in a tunnel). Bringing a person back to the here-and-now may take as little as two minutes or as much as ten or fifteen minutes. Expect a slower than usual response because the person's sense of time may be distorted.

If the person does not respond to any of the measures listed above, say "Listen to me, I am going to take just the tips of your fingers in mine and just hold them, just on the ends of your fingers as you look into my eyes so that I know you are focusing on me [pause to see if there is a response]. That's right, just feel my hands holding the tips of your fingers, now just focus on my face and look at my eyes, and I will know you are back in the present." Once the person can look you in the eye, you can release your hold. Then you can explain, "You 'zoned out' for a little bit [or, had a flashback] but you're okay. Let's do a little bit of exercise, shake out your arms and legs or stretch them to get your body moving." Then help the person identify the trigger for the dissociation or flashback.

## Default of the self

Parts work with the most severely traumatized individuals sometimes faces the difficult situation of a person unable to find a core self. The person feels so influenced by various parts of the self that there seems to be no competent leadership available. This might be a response to current stress or it might be chronic, seemingly life-long. The competing parts are usually striving to deal with past childhood adversity. Their influence on present behavior results in extreme emotion and ineffective action. In the course of parts work, the individual may have identified particular parts and the emotional blending with the parts but then discovers that the present persona is but a part that fails to manage the system of parts.

Then, who is the real self? Therapeutic responses to this challenge might logically include techniques to find the true self. If this fails, one might try to promote one of the more competent parts to a temporary leader position, at least until more trauma therapy relieves enough burdens that the real self can emerge and take charge. The goal is to integrate the system so that all of the parts are on the team with a team leader in charge.

We have followed the technique of the Internal Family Systems Therapy model (Goulding & Schwartz, 2002) to help a person "get into self." Our approach differs only in our limiting the therapist to addressing only the patient and not the part. The following is our instruction to the patient:

> *Identify the part or feeling to focus on in the dialogue process.*
>
> *Locate the part or feeling in, or around, your body.*
>
> *Ask yourself how you feel toward that part or feeling. Be honest with yourself in terms of how you truly feel toward this part or feeling. If you feel anything other than compassion or curiosity toward the part or feeling, then this is your cue that other parts are blending with your true self. If there is another feeling, focus on that feeling and any associated part, acknowledge the feeling, and*

*ask the part to step back. Promise the part that you will later listen to it as well. Be sure to follow through with this promise.*

*Once the blended part has stepped back, repeat step three and take notice of how you feel toward the part or feeling that you identified in step one.*

*Repeat step four, looking for blending from any other parts. If necessary, repeat step five. Continue repeating steps three, four, and five until you are confident that the true self is in charge.*

*When the true self is in control, begin the externalized dialogue process.*

- ### *What is the true self?*

The Instinctual Trauma Response model assumes that a person's self contains a body and two minds with multiple parts. The parts are assumed to be latent mental systems that are experienced as enduring psychophysiological states. The governing mental system is related to the language areas of the dominant cerebral hemisphere, while the latent mental systems could be verbal or nonverbal states of past experience. It would seem that a person's self is the over-arching whole containing the two minds with all of the parts. However, in the IFS Model Richard Schwartz postulates a "true self" that can be differentiated from the parts (Goulding & Schwartz, 2002; Schwartz, 1995). He describes the true self by the eight "C's:" calmness, compassion, curiosity, clarity, confidence, creativity, courage, and connectedness. In this light, the true self would seem to be of a higher order than the brain's mental systems or hemispheres and might suggest a metaphysical entity. That is not the claim of Richard Schwartz, nor is it our assumption. We regard the true self to be the original mental system that arises with the earliest neural network in the fetus. Other mental systems develop with maturation of the brain and under the influence of genes, pains, and gratifications. In practice, we place the true self as the core part in the center of all of the parts of the person. However, after a childhood of adverse experiences, traumatized parts may obscure a person's core part. One essential job of the trauma therapist is to promote access to the true self.

91

# PART 3: TREATMENT OF SPECIFIC SYNDROMES

## *Treatment of Trauma Voices and Command Hallucinations*

Clinicians usually regard auditory hallucinations as symptoms of major mental illness, even though some fifteen percent of non-patient adults admit hearing voices (Young, Bentall, Slade, & Dewey. 1986). Patients often keep their voices secret for fear they will be considered crazy. This is true even when the voices command the person to commit suicide or to kill someone else. People do sometimes obey those commands, and this fact adds urgency to clinical interventions, which usually attempt to suppress the voices by any means available. The common measures involve distracting the person from listening to the voices or medicating the individual to the point that he or she cannot attend to the voices. Electroconvulsive treatment is sometimes done when the voices cannot be stopped with medication. Most treatment efforts are protracted and demoralizing to the person and the end point is usually an uncertain claim that the voices are "gone."

An entirely different approach to dealing with voices is recommended by some clinicians experienced in addressing trauma. Colin Ross (2000) says, "Talk to the voices." Robert Firestone (1997) urges externalizing the suicidal voice. Others describe techniques of externalized dialogue (Holmes & Tinnin, 1995) and working with parts (Schwartz, 1995). These approaches share the notion that inner voices arise from activity of the person's brain and are a part of the person's mind although they speak with some independence. The goal of intervention here is to recruit those voices to the service of the person.

### The nature of hallucinations

We have treated many patients who hear voices. Over half of the trauma patients endorse hallucinations on the assessment questionnaires. Most perceive the voices as originating inside their heads. Inner voices tend to be louder than regular voices and they insistently nag and complain or give a running commentary on a person's behavior. It does not matter about the putative diagnosis of the person. While voices are most likely to be present in dissociative patients, the same kind of voices, behaving in the same way, occur in schizophrenia and bipolar disorder (Ross, 2000). Usually the individual voices are constant companions and recognizable with respect to approximate age and gender. Sometimes there is a single voice, but often, that voice is balanced by another opposed to the intent of the first. More commonly, there are groups of voices—some with prominent roles and some just bit players. There may be the crying from trapped infants or young children. Other cries are of older traumatized selves. When there are young, helpless children, there may be older protectors. There is no limit to that internal world. Voices keep arising as a consequence of specific traumatic experiences.

The patient may hear only one or two voices. This "layer" often contains a commanding voice urging total subjugation and humiliation. It may impel the person to drink or to starve or cut, or it may demand suicide. The patient typically reacts with automatic, trance-like obedience and is saved only by appeals from another voice saying "No," or the intervention of another actual person. After such a crisis, the person may detect other voices in other layers and learn that they are all related to traumas. If the person is able to learn more before once again trying to ignore the voices, there may come a realization that many of these voices are past selves of the person still locked in the trauma that froze their action. Other voices are protectors of young traumatized selves, and some are keepers of the "secret" as commanded by a perpetrator.

## What about schizophrenia?

Certainly, patients with schizophrenia hear voices too. However, it is a fact that they do not hear them as often as dissociative patients do (Kluft, 1997). The fact that people with schizophrenia hear voices "outside" their heads does not help because everyone who hears voices sometimes hear them coming from outside. We think that muffled voices from afar are more characteristic of schizophrenia but we know of no convincing study that looks at the differences between diagnostic groups and their perception of the location of the voices.

In any event, the procedures that we have tested and describe in this book worked just as well for the patients with schizophrenia that we have treated. Their voices are not different. The automatic obedience to the command hallucination is just as easy to change in them as it is in patients with dissociation.

## Specific steps for dealing with voices

### The first step: Making contact with the voice

Imagine talking to John, a man in his thirties, who was discharged a week ago from an inpatient unit. He reports that he feels no better despite taking the many pills prescribed to stop the voice that drove him to the brink of suicide. That voice and others in the background will not leave him alone, and he feels close to obeying the command to stab himself. The more he resists, the stronger the voice becomes. You ask about the voices and learn that he has heard two or three voices for years, and he has made serious attempts to kill himself because a voice wanted that. And right now, because of all this questioning, the voice tells him to get out of your office! You might think of trying to change the subject, but it certainly won't help to ask him to do serial seven's or spell "world" backwards. Instead, you take "the first step."

Announce that you will ask the voice three questions and John is to report what the voice says. "Voice," you say—with some authority—"Are you listening?" Without a pause, John says, "Yes." Without pause, you say, "What do you do for John?" "Nothing," answers the voice. Your third question might be "What do you really want for John?" The voice may give some sneering remark, but the content of the remark does not matter. For John, the mystique of the voice has been removed by hearing it respond to you. In all likelihood, the automatic obedience he had felt toward the voice is now gone. At the least, you have begun to help him see that the voices are generated by his brain.

### The second step: Talking with the voice

You may want to do some talking about voices with John, and it might help to normalize the phenomenon of voices. "Of course, it's normal to hear voices. Everybody does it at night when they dream." However, you do not want to wait too long to persuade John to talk to the voice. It is time for you to step back from a participant role and become a coach for John. You help him externalize his talking to the voice. He talks aloud to the voice, addressing it as "you," or writes a message to the voice, or—much better—video-records his message to the voice. This will be the first of a series of taking turns, each addressing the other as "you" or by name. Now, it is the turn for "Voice" to speak. John may have to speak for the voice at first, but before long Voice will speak for itself, speaking through John. Your coaching will help John develop a dialogue with Voice.

### The third step: Negotiating with the voice

John wants to live. Voice wants John to die. Most commonly, Voice first emerged as a horrified youngster in the shock of a trauma that numbed John's mind and ever since Voice tries to protect John with extreme measures, even to the extreme of death as escape. Once John is coached to search out what Voice really wants (in this case, escape for John) he can begin some negotiation. What if John could persuade Voice that he no longer had to carry the burden of rescue? What might John do to help Voice shift to a less extreme role? The answers bring problem solving and agreements and soon (after four to six externalized dialogues) John and Voice may have difficulty differentiating themselves from each other.

You have helped John remove the intimidating mask of a god, demon, or supernatural entity from the voice. At the same time, you have reified the voice by talking to it and encouraging John to talk to it as if it were another person. It is counterintuitive to risk increasing the differentiation of the voice in a dialogue when you know that John needs to own the voice as a part of him. Our experience with many externalized dialogues like John's has convinced us that the natural outcome of externalized dialogue is de-differentiation and diminished dissociation.

## Voices have quirks

There are certain quirks that characterize the majority of voices. It helps the clinician to know about these quirks and to be able to take advantage of them.

### Voices are gullible

Most voices come from latent mental systems that occupy the realm of the nonverbal or subconscious mind and are influenced by the nature of that milieu. The typical behavior of nonverbal mentation is first and foremost one of "followership." The syntax for nonverbal thought is normally provided by the language centers of the verbal mind (Broca's area, Wernicke's area). That syntax includes identity, time and sequence, volition, reality monitoring, and role assignment. When trauma, anesthesia, drugs, or disease disables the verbal mind, the nonverbal mind might be adrift. The dissociated states of self with their voices may be desperate for leadership and for the missing elements of syntax. The practical consequence for voices that represent latent mental systems frozen in past traumas is that their identity and roles are ripe for reframing by the individual's present verbal mind. Our experience is that the externalized dialogue is a practical vehicle for communicating with those voices, influencing them, and reframing their identity and roles.

### Voices hear voices

When someone negotiates with a voice that urges suicide and finally gains agreement to pursue a different option, keep in mind that this may not be the end of the matter. There may be another suicidal voice ready to fill the role vacated by the first. Separate negotiations with different voices may be necessary.

- *Case example*

  *Twenty-seven-year-old Melissa seemed to have accomplished a successful video dialogue with the part of herself that believed she was horribly fat even at 96 pounds. As the days passed, it was clear that Melissa was still starving herself. She did some more dialogue, and her search exposed another part that took over the anorexic role. Later, she had to negotiate with a third one who made the same exhortations to starve herself.*

### The best defense is a strong offense

The fiercer the voices sound, the meeker they are in the end. People may be terrified of their voices and fearful for the safety of the therapist if that fierce voice "gets out." Once engaged in dialogue, the voice becomes simply another aspect of the person and, more often than not, a younger aspect. We did have one person whose four-year-old part hit Linda without warning and in full view of the treatment team and her mother. This episode, and our experience with younger parts convince us that parts developed around four years of age are the most difficult to persuade to yield to the leadership of older parts or self.

### Voices can be wise

Some voices become helpers by providing a clear-headed response to the negative voices. Some voices exemplify a wise archetype or a role of "inner-self-helper" described in the literature on dissociative disorders (Allison, 1974). That helpful voice can be called on during the course of therapy using the externalized dialogue process.

## Using voices in treatment

### Suicide

Most suicidal persons experience an inner voice urging suicide (Firestone, 1997, 2001). Such voices come to dominate their thinking to the point that they feel no choice. The most effective intervention occurs when the person engages in an externalized dialogue with the suicidal voice. In most cases, this empowers the part that wants to live; the person can make a deal with the suicidal part to try another option. If a part cannot take a stand against suicide, there is still a possibility of finding another inner voice that will debate both the voice urging suicide and the person suffused with that idea. If, however, no part can be found to speak for life then hospital confinement and protection by other people becomes necessary.

### Self-mutilation

When someone cuts one's self or deliberately harms the body in some other way, he or she is usually aware of an internal polarity of opinion about the act. It makes a real difference to examine that polarity using an externalized dialogue. The voices that argue for or against the act are usually several. A number of dialogues may be required with a variety of positions to be negotiated. It may be difficult to manage all the debate before the person has succeeded in processing the earliest of the traumas. Trauma processing and repeated dialogue go hand-in-hand in these cases.

- *Case example*

*Ann was a 48-year-old woman who requested help with "being very afraid and having negative, self-destructive, and bothersome thoughts." Nearing the end of her first week of two in the clinic she had processed two early traumas and identified eight parts, one of which is the Self-Abuser. She chose to write her externalized dialogues. This is a dialogue between her "Self" and a twelve-year-old part, "Self-Abuser." She used her left hand when writing for the part.*

*Self: Please tell me about that urge to cut your wrists.*

*Self-Abuser: I want to cut my wrists. I feel miserable.*

*Self: I am sorry to hear that you feel lousy right now. Tell me what's going on, if you can.*

*Self-Abuser: Mom just called and I was short with her. She tries to act like she is only supportive and she bothers me.*

*Self: I know what you mean. I told her when she asked how we were doing that I was hanging in there and she said that's "not enough...I hope they are helping you there." I explained that I am working my tail off and didn't need to hear her anxiety or lectures. She immediately said she had "no anxiety." Then after we hung up I felt guilty and I think that's when you popped up, right?*

*Self-Abuser: Yes, you were short with her, and she has Alzheimer's so I punished you by thoughts of cutting your wrists.*

*Self: Thanks for telling me that. You know I would never actually cut them, though, but I see your logic and point. Can we negotiate some type of deal for future times?*

*Self-Abuser: What deal?*

*Self: Well, just an idea but maybe I can try just a little harder to avoid talking in a cross or angry way to her and in exchange you cannot punish me so much or often. Can you understand that she confuses and worries me?*

**Self-Abuser:** *That's your problem.*

**Self:** *It is, and as team leader I want, really want, to fix this. Because I/we are worth it! No matter what we've said or done before, I/we did the best I could. And so did Mom, and maybe you can help me remember that? Is that reasonable a request?*

**Self-Abuser:** *I think you ought to have that down by now.*

**Self:** *I hear you and agree, but unfortunately (or perhaps fortunately) I am only now really learning. You know things have changed with Mom, and it got me off-kilter. It's not meant to be an excuse, but trust me, it's the truth.*

**Self-Abuser:** *I don't like you.*

**Self:** *I know. Can that ever change?*

**Self-Abuser:** *Yes, it can. Keep being true to yourself and stop fucking worrying about what others think.*

**Self:** *Wow – that is <u>Good</u>, <u>Great</u> advice. You are a smart and wise girl even at twelve. You came through it, though, and screw those brats like Shelley, Trish, and Jean who rejected and made fun of you. They were jealous, threatened, or just mean spirited.*

 **Self-Abuser:** *Yes, I like you better now.*

**Self:** *Oh, I am so glad to hear that! Because I love you, twelve-year-old girl, and I may get "bothered" by some of your thoughts, but I <u>Love</u> you and you are cool.*

**Self-Abuser:** *Thanks, I will try to stop punishing you. You don't really deserve it.*

**Self:** *That sounds GREAT—you really are kind and wise. You were not mean. I know I/we did give Rosie and Dawn a hard time, but we can pray and ask God for forgiveness, God and Jesus.*

**Self-Abuser:** *I don't think they like me.*

**Self:** *What make you say that?*

**Self-Abuser:** *Because my ideas of self-harm are sinful.*

***Self:*** *Well, so many people have those kinds of ideas and some people actually act on them. You don't. Maybe just try to be a little less harsh on me/others, OK?*

***Self-Abuser:*** *Okay— goodnight.*

## *Treatment of PTSD*

The structural model of dissociation (Van der Hart, et al., 2006) assigns simple PTSD to the level of primary dissociation in which the reality-based, *Apparently Normal Personality* (ANP) functions independently of the *Emotional Personality* (EP). The Instinctual Trauma Response model understands this as a limitation of transcallosal access between verbal and nonverbal cerebral hemispheres. The limitation seems to be maintained by trauma phobia, involving fear of reliving the traumatic memories (Van der Hart, et al., 2006). Successful trauma therapy resolves trauma phobia and establishes normal transcallosal access to the hemispheres.

Before normal access is achieved, the limitation to interhemispheric communication can be bypassed by various measures of externalization. Verbal information issuing from the left hemisphere can be spoken aloud and received externally by the right hemisphere while nonverbal information can be drawn or shown through sculpture or other creative arts and received externally by the left hemisphere. Our term for this is *callosal bypass.* A callosal bypass in trauma therapy for PTSD and dissociative disorders is achieved by hypnosis, graphic narrative processing, externalized dialogue, art making, play therapy, and parts mapping.

### Acute stress symptoms

Trauma phobia and alexithymia signal the presence of dissociated traumatic memory. Following a traumatic event, the individual's retraction of consciousness and emotional constriction may avert the emergence of traumatic imprints or dissociated mental states for varying periods.

Sometimes the acute stress is severe enough to arouse survival instincts and weaken cerebral dominance with resulting intrusions of the traumatic memory and survival instincts such as fight/flight, freeze, or depersonalization symptoms. These symptoms merit the diagnosis of acute stress syndrome. If they persist beyond one month, they will merit the diagnosis of post-traumatic stress disorder (PTSD).

## Simple PTSD

Both acute stress symptoms and PTSD following Type 1 trauma can be successfully treated by narrative processing of the identified trauma(s) along with externalized dialogue between the present person and the dissociated traumatized self. In simple PTSD, the troubling latent mental system consists of the self one was when overcome by the trauma. The dissociative symptoms of these patients are usually limited to flashbacks and nightmares. However, there usually is a significant trauma phobia that gives rise to symptoms of avoidance and arousal.

The narrative processing for simple PTSD can be accomplished by the graphic narrative alone—without the need for hypnosis or guided imagery—in individual or group sessions. The externalized dialogue can be conveniently accomplished by written dialogue, which is usually read aloud by the patient or therapist and it can be done in the group setting. More extensive parts work is required for complex PTSD symptoms.

## Combat PTSD

The dissociative symptoms of combat PTSD go beyond the flashbacks and nightmares of simple PTSD. Most patients with combat PTSD hear voices (Holmes & Tinnin, 1995), many of which are command hallucinations urging suicide. The veterans often identify the commands as coming from a warrior part of themselves that was specialized for combat. This fits secondary dissociation in terms of the structural dissociation model. The inner warrior is a latent mental system dedicated to the combat mission.

Our treatment of combat veterans often begins with externalized dialogue because of the urgent need to deal with command hallucinations (see above, *Treatment of Command Hallucinations*). Once this is done, we turn to sequential processing of traumatic experiences before the combat trauma. This is particularly helpful for combat veterans because of their typically high trauma phobia and resistance to talking about their combat experiences. With success in processing the earlier traumas, the patients can approach the combat traumas with confidence.

Some of these patients are burdened with the pessimism of victim mythology. They will often hear more than one voice. Treatment in these cases will require parts work to relieve the victim mythology.

- ### *Case example*

*Steve was a 54-year-old combat veteran of Vietnam. He had been a First Lieutenant platoon leader exposed to a high level of combat including a gunshot wound to his left arm. When he returned to the states, he was filled with grim determination to succeed in his job of geologist. He succeeded despite an addiction to alcohol.*

*His self-driven course was broken when he attended a reunion of his regiment and talked with some veterans of his platoon. They told him a story of his bravery in combat that had disappeared from his memory. The platoon was overrun by the Viet Cong, and Steve had led the remaining men through to survival, killing many of the enemy.*

*Steve's reaction seemed paradoxical. He began having nightmares of the experience, which he visualized repeatedly as a waking dream. He had an overwhelming sense of sadness and guilt, feeling he did not do enough. He felt he was a coward. His physician referred him for urgent treatment at the trauma center.*

*The treatment was a perfect fit for him. He was able to use his hypnotic Hidden Observer to thoroughly study the trauma and see that he had been in a prolonged altered state of consciousness, during which he functioned on a high level as a soldier. He drew out a graphic narrative that unveiled all of the verbal and nonverbal elements of the story and immediately brought closure to the memory.*

*Steve's performance in combat is a variant of automatic obedience that we term automatic pilot. Soldiers, as well as first responders and emergency medical personnel, have over-learned their skills in repeated high-stress training sessions. The instinctual automatic obedience state is available in a trauma to sustain the automatic pilot actions.*

## Complex PTSD

Complex PTSD is also known as "disorders of extreme stress, not otherwise specified" [or DESNOS] (Van der Hart, et al., 2006, pp. 112-113). These patients appear to have characterological disturbances with dissociative alterations in attention or consciousness (Van der Hart, Nijenhuis, & Steele, 2005). This would represent secondary dissociation in the structural dissociation theory. They usually have suffered extensive childhood trauma or prolonged trauma during adulthood such as domestic violence or captivity.

The treatment of complex PTSD includes the narrative trauma processing and externalized dialogue for dissociation, but the work on early traumas and the parts work for victim mythology is more extensive than that for simple PTSD. Our approach to complex PTSD is identical to our treatment of dissociative disorders.

## *Treatment of Dissociative Disorders*

### Dissociative symptoms

Dissociative symptoms arise from more complex post-traumatic disturbances of dual brain dynamics. They involve interference with consciousness in three ways: interruption of consciousness, alteration of consciousness, and displacement of consciousness.

Dissociative interruption of consciousness occurs in both PTSD and dissociative disorders. In PTSD, it is flashbacks. In dissociative disorders, it may also involve auditory hallucinations or other manifestations of latent mental systems in the form of ego states or parts.

Dissociative alteration of consciousness results in trance states, depersonalization (altered states, out-of-body experiences), derealization (sense of unreality of self or surroundings), or amnesia. Displacement of consciousness occurs when a competing latent ego displaces one's usual personality as in dissociative identity disorder.

### DDNOS

The most commonly treated dissociative disorder is dissociative disorder not otherwise specified (DDNOS). DSM-IV-TR,

(American Psychiatric Association, 2000) defines six categories of DDNOS: atypical dissociative identity disorder, derealization unaccompanied by depersonalization in adults, states of dissociation due to captivity and intensive coercive persuasion, dissociative or possession trance, alteration of consciousness due to a medical condition, and, finally, Ganser syndrome (the giving of approximated answers to questions, such as "two plus two equals five"). We will focus on the first and largest category, *atypical DID*.

The majority of these patients complain of voices, depersonalization, derealization, and impairment in work and personal relationships. Aggressive and suicidal impulses are frequent, as is self-harming behavior. They differ from DID patients only by the absence of alter personalities that displace consciousness and amnesia for the time occupied by alter personalities.

The primary tasks, objectives, phases, and goals of our trauma therapy are the same for PTSD and dissociative disorders. The more complex disorders require more parts work, but the approach of therapist relating to the patient and the patient relating to parts holds throughout. Another aspect that is the same for dissociative disorders as well as for PTSD is that in the absence of dissociative regression, trauma processing begins during the first phase of treatment and begins with preverbal trauma processing. The patient's trust in the process and in the therapist develops in the wake of successful trauma processing. As the dissociative patient becomes more experienced in the processing and parts work, he or she increasingly leads the treatment. The procedural nature of the trauma therapy makes it easier to learn and to apply independently. The graphic narrative processing is a procedure as is the externalized dialogue. Increasingly internal dialogue and parts work is becoming procedural.

This method does not depend on relationship psychotherapy or corrective emotional experience. Nor does it require desensitization or cognitive reprocessing. It is not directed to merely coping with symptoms. Trust is an important element, but it is not trust in the therapist. The trust to be developed is an inner trust between the individual's self and parts. The therapist shows the patient how to study the traumatic events without reliving them and how to bring closure to the nonverbal memory. The therapist coaches the patient in parts work. It is not necessary for the patient to attach to the therapist.

- ***Case example***

*This example is in the form of a treatment summary sent to the hometown therapist at termination of the two-week intensive treatment.*

*Carol, age 44, completed a two-week Intensive Individual Trauma Treatment program. She was able to process a number of major traumas related to her early life and to begin to make some sense of her dissociative symptoms and disturbing flashbacks and body memories. Judging from her response to our program, we feel she has an excellent prognosis for recovering from her trauma-related symptoms. However, she will still require weekly individual outpatient psychotherapy in order to continue working on those issues we did not have time to treat.*

*Carol processed the following major events from her early life using hypnosis, art therapy (the graphic narrative), and the externalized dialogue process:*

o Severe fetal distress at week 28 that required an emergency C-section;

o Being suffocated and strangled twice by her mother when she was about two or three years old;

o Being stabbed in the genitals by her mother when approximately 12 months old;

o Being sexually abused repeatedly by her mother and her father and being raped by her demented grandfather;

o Witnessing her mother attack her father with a weapon (and thinking he was dead and that her mother was going to kill Carol and then kill herself).

*During the processing of these traumas, Carol had difficulty staying fully present. We used music and grounding techniques to help her stay in the here-and-now. As the two-week program went on, Carol found herself*

106

*gradually but increasingly able to tolerate being in her body.*

*Carol will have to be the judge as to whether the above named events have been thoroughly processed. She can tell if more work needs to be done by whether she continues to have flashbacks about them. If there is an important detail that was omitted from the story, she can add it to the graphic narrative. Then Carol and her therapist can review the video recording of that particular trauma, stop the tape where the omitted detail belongs, talk about the detail, and then finish reviewing the video.*

*In individual psychotherapy sessions, we discussed the following themes that were woven into her life:*

o The origin of her eating disorder and her need to make certain she had a supply of food at all times;

o Her inability to do adequate self-repair because her mother was a principal perpetrator;

o Her emotional numbness [which originated in the freeze] and depersonalization [which originated in the altered state of consciousness];

o Her suicidal feelings and her eating disorder as being connected to the particular traumas, not separate disorders.

*The most notable accomplishments Carol made were:*

o Recognizing the existence of "parts" that both originated in and were stuck in specific traumatic events and understanding that these parts contaminated her present-day feelings;

o Discovering the source of her feelings of depersonalization;

o Learning how to shift a trauma from "present tense" flashbacks and to "past tense" historical events;

o Learning how to use the externalized dialogue to identify and deal with troublesome memories and impulses (such as overeating).

*Using the process of the externalized dialogue Carol can:*

o Check in with the parts when she experiences emotional flashbacks;

o Negotiate internal agreements;

o Determine the "unfinished" business;

o Soothe the younger parts and give them more adult skills.

*We were able to develop a map of Carol's "parts" with each part corresponding to her age at the time of significant traumas. [Carol has the original "stickies" we used to make the map as well as digital copies of the different iterations.] She made a long list about the different aspects of herself ("the closet ones, the hyper-alert ones, the sexaholics, friend of...", etc.). As we came to know more about Carol's parts we concluded that she does indeed merit a diagnosis of dissociative disorder, not otherwise specified (DDNOS); however, with more work, she will find that her parts will become more like present-day self. Her system has already begun to shift, and the map she did on the last day at ITT showed greater cooperation and communication.*

*Recommendations for Carol:*

o Review the traumas processed at ITT;

o Review the dialogues and summarize significant themes;

o Process the remaining traumas; and

o Allot regular time for self-repair.

*Carol has all the video recordings, the written dialogues, and the graphic narratives (drawings of the traumas) that she made as a part of the trauma processing. We recommend that she review selected portions of this material during future therapy sessions. She can choose those events and dialogues that are the most important to her. It is imperative that she continue the externalized dialogue; this is her best opportunity to bring to the surface the issues that relate to her emotional life in childhood.*

*There are other later traumas to be processed. Carol now has tools for telling these stories (the graphic narrative) and for doing the externalized dialogue with those parts of her that are stuck in the past.*

*Carol needs to allot time for self-repair. She had an intellectual understanding of many of her problems but had been unable to have compassion for herself until her parts could hear and comprehend what happened to her.*

*We will ask Carol to repeat our testing protocol at one week, three months, and six months in order to collect data for our outcome study. We told her that some ups and downs are to be expected as she continues her recovery. We are available for follow-up sessions or for a telephone consultation with her therapist.*

*Our staff found Carol to be extremely motivated, eager to work, and able to give us excellent feedback on her responses to our techniques so we could make adjustments in our pacing and focus of the program. Below are her assessment scores on our trauma profile:*

|                | TRS | DRS | DES | TAS | SCL | IES |
|----------------|-----|-----|-----|-----|-----|-----|
| Pre-Treatment  | 32  | 35  | 33  | 87  | 122 | 20  |
| Post-Treatment | 65  | 28  | 12  | 81  | 63  | 10  |

## Treatment of dissociative identity disorder

Dissociative identity disorder (DID) usually begins in early childhood with the experience of Type 2 trauma, commonly child battering or sexual abuse, but may follow repeated medical or surgical trauma. It may also have an adult onset following prolonged captivity or torture (Spiegel & Cardena, 1991). It is frequently experienced by the victim as being crazy and may be concealed from others. The DES scores of our patients diagnosed with DID are usually above 50.

The individual may be aware only of lost time and may not remember the experiences of altered identity. Often the person has a secret awareness of internal dialogue between other selves. The DSM criteria for the diagnosis include switching of personalities and amnesia for at least some of the experience of altered identity.

The other personalities of the person with DID may be male, female, child, or adult. Commonly there are alter related to specific phases of the trauma response (Nijenhuis, et al., 1998). For example, there may be a personality related to the fight/flight response that experiences perpetual alarm and urges to escape. Another personality might be related to the freeze state and experience sensory anesthesia and emotional numbing. The automatic obedience experienced in the Instinctual Trauma Response may determine the behavior of the personality with traumaphilia (drawn to repetition of the trauma) who is repeatedly victimized (Kluft, 1990). A variety of personalities develop from the altered state of consciousness, such as the depersonalized out-of-body self, the zombie personality, or an object or animal related to a dissociative fantasy or an object of fixated vision (for example, a doll stared at during the abuse). A personality with compulsive washing may be related to the self-repair state.

Some alter personalities are locked into the trauma of their origin and frozen in time. There may be child states suspended in perpetual distress while other child personalities are ignorant of any trauma. Frequently there is one personality who mirrors the perpetrator (Ross, 1997).

The alternation of personalities in DID is not simply one personality replacing the other. The alter personalities co-exist as concurrent multiple streams of experience. Their activities are experienced at different levels of consciousness, and they may communicate with each other outside of consciousness. Their communication may be experienced by the dominant conscious personality as auditory hallucinations.

The individual sometimes experiences the alter personalities as dwelling within an internal mental realm that may be represented as a mental architecture or landscape. The imagined place might be a house with rooms designated for the alter personalities or a complex cavern with many passages. When these scenes are drawn on paper the depiction changes over time as the dissociative condition changes.

Because the multiple personalities are carried by one person, the question arises, who is the patient? Some therapists relate to each personality as an individual patient with unique problems to be resolved. A way to avoid this pitfall is to use the video camera and replay in a manner that permits the patient to deal directly with the alter personalities while the therapist relates only to the patient. We relate to a single individual, the primary personality or the "host" personality. We resist being drawn into therapeutic relationships with multiple alter personalities who may vie for our attention. The video dialogue procedure makes it possible for issues between the "primary" personality and the "alters" to be handled by the parts rather than by the therapist.

Usually the alter personalities are asked to not participate in the first phase of the trauma processing. The alters can go to a "safe place." The hypnotic narration is done by the Hidden Observer rather than a personality. The alter personalities are to participate in the trauma processing when the recording is reviewed.

The entire course of treatment for the person with DID is simplified by the use of video dialogue. The use of externalized dialogue makes it possible for the patient to retain primary responsibility for the communication between personalities.

DID patients often become adept at processing traumas by graphic narration, so that after the first few experiences of hypnotic trauma narration, the graphic narrative becomes the primary means of traumatic memory processing.

### Treat dissociative regression first

Dissociative regression occurs as a complication of trauma and is frequently seen in dissociative disorders. In this form of regression, a person loses the normal capacity for self-regulation because of diminished cerebral dominance (Tinnin, 1989). The primary personality may experience a weakening of identity with a loss of mental unity or self-sameness over time. The patient may lose a reliable sense of time (including duration and sequence) or lack the capacity for volition or will. He or she might experience a diffusion of self-boundary and have difficulty distinguishing self from other. When dissociative regression is present, one often has difficulty with verbal symbolization and may become literal-minded. The processing of traumatic memories usually must be deferred until the regression is reversed.

The treatment of dissociative regression proceeds as described above (pages 40-43) but may take more time in the case of DID.

## Treatment contract

Trauma therapy begins by establishing ground rules about the therapeutic relationship and the procedures to be used. Our approach is usually a team effort with different therapists conducting the different treatment procedures. Even when a single therapist does most of the work with an individual patient, the nature of the therapeutic relationship is less personal and exclusive than in conventional therapy. The dominant personality of the patient conducts the communication with the alter personalities with advice and coaching from the therapist. The therapist does not enter into individual therapeutic relationships with the alter personalities and tries to avoid direct communication with them.

These ground rules are discussed and demonstrated in action by having the dominant personality talk out loud (into the video camera) to the alter personalities in turn, each time playing back the speech and watching it on behalf of the alter personality. The person then "speaks for" the alter personality (who is expected to take over and speak out), again talking aloud and recording the speech for the dominant personality to watch on replay. This initial video dialogue focuses on the issue of participation and avoidance of sabotage in the treatment. The dominant personality negotiates and tries to win agreement by the others to cooperate and not interfere.

## Narrative trauma processing

The first step of the trauma work is to gain access to the traumatic memory, including both verbal memory and wordless images, and to describe it in the form of a verbal narrative. Most patients succeed with the help of guided imagery. The trauma scenes are narrated by the Hidden Observer who is not an alter personality but, rather, a naturally occurring dissociative point of view (Hilgard, 1977) that permits an emotionally detached scrutiny. The presence of amnesic barriers between alter personalities and the primary personality does not impede the view of the Hidden Observer.

We recommend that the first processing focus on a preverbal trauma such as a known illness or surgical procedure. It is not necessary to have any preverbal memories of such an event.

Alternatively, the session can process a potentially traumatic birth experience as visualized by the Hidden Observer.

Using guided imagery, the entire narrative is completed in a single ninety-minute session. The session is video recorded, and the recording is reviewed by the dominant personality with full participation of the alter personalities in the presence of the therapist. That second session may also be video recorded to include the soundtrack of the first tape and any discussion or elaboration of the narrative. This recording may be used for homework by the patient unless the review was interrupted by excessive emotion or dissociation. In that case, the session is repeated and a second recursive recording is made for the homework review. The patient's task is to review and study the recording with the goal of owning the narrative as personal history.

We routinely conduct a graphic narration to complete the trauma processing. The objective of this is to construct a graphic narrative of the Instinctual Trauma Response that includes the essential phases and to transform the nonverbal imagery to a verbal narrative.

### Parts work for dissociation

The externalized dialogue between the patient in the present and the part in the trauma commences after the narrative processing is completed. The objective is to make sure that any traumatically dissociated latent mental system or personality is liberated from the trauma and invited into the present life of the person. The person will also recruit those alter personalities who were developed for special purposes, aside from dealing with trauma, to become integrated in present life.

The alter personalities in dissociative identity disorder sometimes develop complicated systems that resist integration. A common motivation for this resistance is to protect the person from memory of horrific traumatic experiences. This motivation is diminished by using the Hidden Observer as narrator. Other reasons for resistance involve the emotional investment in the community of alter personalities with their alliances around privilege and power. Some alters fear being "killed off." The system of alter personalities may regard the person as too damaged and too weak to manage alone in the seemingly dangerous world. Alter personalities sometimes resist exchanging their extreme protective roles for ones that are more realistic.

The solution to such resistances lies in the persistence of the primary personality in communicating and negotiating externally. Internal communication is not sufficient. Agreements made internally should be restated or written externally.

The goal of treatment is for the person to achieve a continuous memory and the cooperation of alter personalities in conscious awareness. If alter personalities continue to be differentiated from the primary person they can take reasonable roles as team members with the identified person as the team leader.

### Externalizing of parts in play therapy with children and adults

Children are able to externalize their traumatized inner parts spontaneously in play with toys and puppets. Dissociative adults can also use puppets to externalize alter personalities (Gerity, 1999). This approach is particularly useful for the person having difficulty accepting the existence of dissociated parts. In the beginning, the therapist might speak for one or another puppet part to encourage the patient to engage in give-and-take communication with the part.

### Intensive trauma therapy for DID

The conventional outpatient psychotherapy for these patients presents extraordinary problems. The patient may be chronically suicidal and the therapy dominated by seemingly perpetual crisis. These remarkable therapists that do this work find themselves bombarded and often struggling to manage these crises. Stalemates in therapy may seem endless. Actual trauma processing seems impossible. It makes a great difference when a therapist has available an inpatient program that specializes in emergency trauma therapy for these patients. Our intensive outpatient program (described below) endeavors to provide this intervention without hospitalization and without medications. The goal is to provide a marathon trauma therapy of two weeks that will help the patient surmount the block in treatment and return to the referring therapist with renewed capacity for progress.

*The following describes in detail a two-week treatment
(Monday through Friday, seven hours per day) of a person
with a diagnosis of dissociative identity disorder. Doris
was a 50-year-old unemployed health care worker who was
in treatment with a trained trauma therapist and had
attended sessions twice weekly for about one-and-a-half
years. She had identified many named alter personalities.
She experienced them as existing on two intrapsychic
levels, an upper and lower level connected by a tunnel. The
lower level held her trauma memories, and the upper level
held the emotions. In the lower level, she was aware of a
fierce alter named "Jude," two "Bad Girls" and 30 babies
(in 6 bubbles that contained 5 babies each). The upper
level contained "Dot" who is very strong, very burdened
and tired but has overall control. It also contained "Stu"
who is a feminine male, "Chris" who is five, and "Judy"
and "Jan" (both young girls).*

*Doris recounted the stalemate in therapy that led to her
coming to our trauma center for treatment and then
expressed her concerns about how triggering this treatment
would be. More specifically, she worried about the fierce
"Jude "coming out because he had not been out in some
time. He has a foul mouth and was aggressive, both
physically and verbally. He wanted to cut people up and
throw them into a river. When "Jude" made an
appearance, Doris did not have any memory of that time.*

*"Chris" is also someone she was concerned about because
he liked to cut and see blood. He was also obsessed with
fire and had tried to get Doris to put her hand in a fire in
order to feel. Doris reported that she and "Dot" did a good
job resisting his many urges to die (by overdosing on pills,
pulling out in front of a truck, sitting in the closed garage
with the motor on), which came over her periodically. "Stu"
does not agree with suicide and serves as a protector along
with "Dot."*

*She shared that going deep down into her system was very
ugly because of the childhood memories involving her*

*parents, some from the first three years of her life. Her coming to the trauma center had been like saying those memories were real and true. Therefore, although she realized how freeing this process could be, she dreaded that truth.*

Doris had become acquainted with two of the staff members by telephone during the screening process and she had self-administered the DES, DRS, and TRS via the clinic website prior to coming in. She was scheduled for two five-day weeks.

### Week 1, Day 1

*During her first morning, she met with the five-person treatment team. She completed the panel of self-administered questionnaires (SCL-45, TAS, and IES) and learned about the Instinctual Trauma Response and the treatment procedures she would experience.*

*The afternoon was devoted to her introductory experience of the basic procedures: guided imagery, graphic narrative, and externalized dialogue. Her introduction to guided imagery focused on her evoked perception of her birth, which she understood as uncomplicated. The family circumstances, however, were complicated by her father's conviction that another man sired her.*

*In the guided imagery after the initial relaxation, she imagined herself stepping out of her body and viewing herself through the eyes of an impassive Hidden Observer. As the Hidden Observer, she pictured her mother in the hospital delivery room giving birth. She visualized the baby's startle on emerging from the birth canal and her fight/flight reaction of screaming while being handled and watched the baby lapse into a prolonged freeze state. The baby was wheeled into the nursery without being returned to her mother. She noted the absence of a maternal gaze and the failure of bonding between mother and child. Finally, the baby was welcomed home by her grandmother with a loving gaze.*

*The next procedure was the graphic narrative processing in which she drew a series of pictures illustrating the birth story generated by the guided imagery. She was organized and rapid in her drawings, which she did entirely in pencil without color. She combined the verbal narrative of her guided imagery with the nonverbal story of the Instinctual Trauma Response and was able to remain grounded throughout.*

*She felt herself beginning to dissociate during the therapist's re-presentation of the graphic narrative but she managed to ground herself by fingering a grounding stone. She felt emotionally moved by the re-presentation and she gained a sense of avowal and closure to the birth story.*

*There was not enough time to include the externalized dialogue procedure, so it was temporarily deferred, and she joined the entire treatment team for the final half-hour wrap-up of the day. All agreed that she had done well in her first day of treatment.*

**Day 2**

*During the "morning rounds," Doris reported that it was difficult to get used to being in the hotel room alone but she slept well for the most part and felt well in the morning. She did experience a nightmare that consisted of feeling closed in or stuck in something, which caused her to wake up feeling panicked. However, she was able to return to sleep. This was an improvement from the past when she would scream and wake up everyone in the house. She slept a total of only 4-and-a-half hours but reported this to be typical.*

*She reported feeling shocked after the re-presentation yesterday by how much she seemed to remember. She connected this story to the emphasis she placed on eye contact with her children once she became a mother. She decided that the baby in yesterday's story was the "Dot" part of her.*

*Day 2's guided imagery session processed a pre-verbal story of witnessing domestic violence between her parents. The baby was only a few months old, wrapped up in a blanket and placed in a drawer, and neglected by her mother and father. The family dog brought the baby out of her instinctual freeze reaction by licking her face, and her*

117

*grandmother eventually came and rescued her from the situation. She was able to identify each phase of the Instinctual Trauma Response.*

*She still felt detached from the baby after completing the graphic narrative. The story was re-presented, and afterward she concluded that the baby in the story was also "Dot." Doris attempted a written dialogue with the baby, but started to rub her forehead, put her hands over her face, put her head down, and said she was getting a headache. She reported there was interference from "Jude." She was asked to write down the thoughts in her head. She wanted "Jude" to go away. Finally, "Dot" had to tell him to go away. Doris described "Jude" as a very powerful part, based in fear. He was protective of the babies, but not very nurturing. She did not want to do any more dialoguing or go "down there" [to the lower level of her intrapsychic system] any more. She said she was tired and then repeated "I'm sorry" many times for letting "Jude" come up.*

*During the wrap-up she read aloud her incomplete dialogue and was reassured by the team that she was doing well. Doris reported that her strong part, "Dot," has always been there. She was 23 years old and seemed tired of all the work she was doing. The treatment team concluded that Doris knew a lot about her system. However, she was controlled by her parts rather than the other way around.*

**Day 3**

*Doris came into the session feeling very unsuccessful, and doubtful the treatment was going to work. She also shared that this might be the only place where she could talk freely about her system and we don't think she's crazy*

*She tried to use video dialogue for the externalized dialogue with the baby but decided she preferred written dialogue. She succeeded in the written dialogue and learned that the baby was actually "Dee." She was happy with this information, as it had answered some disturbing question she had about her system.*

118

*The guided imagery processed a pre-verbal story of neglect by her father and sexual abuse by her father's friend, Harry. Her father, an alcoholic, was left to take care of "Baby Doris," but instead gave her beer. Later his friends came over, and one of them, Harry, performed oral sex on her after changing her diaper. Doris was also able to see that when her mother returned home later that night, she provided Doris with the necessities that she needed, such as milk and a clean diaper. However, it was also apparent that the infant lacked attachment to her mother and was desperately searching for it.*

*Doris completed the graphic narrative of the guided imagery session. She reported that during this session "Dot" was able to stay with her. "Dot" seemed to be letting go and seeing she might not have to do everything. "Jude" was also quiet during this process. She started the process, but did not want to draw the picture illustrating the abuse. After a short review of why it was important, she said, "This is what we need to do" and persisted with the drawing. There was a big smile on her face as she drew the final self-repair picture.*

*During the re-presentation of the graphic narrative, she held a dog puppet for grounding. Afterwards, she reported that she had to gather herself to watch but was present and heard the whole thing. She said it was easier than doing the drawings.*

*She started the written externalized dialogue with the baby as she had learned to do, using her left hand to write the baby's message and her right for the observing self. Initially, she had difficulty writing with her left hand because she said the baby was trying to slant in one direction and she was trying to slant in another. Eventually though, she completed a dialogue in which the baby said she wanted to die during that time and that her parents did not know how to love or care for anyone but themselves. She had questions for the adult about what would happen next and where she would be living. The baby also said that she wanted to use all of the words she could think of to describe how nice she felt to finally be free.*

119

*In the wrap-up session, her presentation and demeanor were drastically different than they had been in the morning. The treatment team felt that Doris showed she could be motherly and nurturing to the infant parts of herself and that it came naturally to her.*

**Day 4**

*The guided imagery session involved a trauma at age three when her father kicked her and her dog. She also studied the discord between her parents and grandparents.*

*When she began the graphic narrative, she realized that the proportions in her drawing were off. She said that one of her parts was taking over the drawing and she was not sure which one, although she suspected it was "Dee" because she was young and did not understand the rules of drawing. Doris determined that the part of her that was a good artist was not participating much. She added that she was not interfering but she also was not contributing.*

*Once she had completed the graphic narrative, re-presentation, and externalized dialogue she concluded she had freed three exiled babies in the lower portion of her system, and it appeared that "Jude" was not protesting.*

**Day 5**

*In the morning check-in, Doris reported that she did a lot of writing the previous night and said she could now recognize who was writing. She was scared of "Jude" before but now she felt sorry for him and hoped that negotiation could help him. She reported that she felt changed since Wednesday and that her husband even noticed a change in her during their telephone conversations. She also said that dissociation had been difficult for everyone in her system, but now she had a word for it. She had read up on it and she was no longer afraid of it.*

*She processed a lengthy story of her long-term sexual and physical abuse by the husband of her father's niece when Doris was between four-months and ten-years-old. She said this had gotten easier for her and she was learning better what questions to ask.*

**Week 2, Day 6,**

*Doris reported that her husband had come into town over the weekend and she "freaked him out." She had an experience of dissociation and what seemed like a panic attack while the two of them were in a store. Doris described this panic attack as everything getting small and dark and feeling like the air was being sucked out of her. She also said that part of her delighted in scaring her husband in that way. At the same time though, she felt sorry for not being able to show him how she had improved. She said that the low she experienced on Saturday, when this occurred, was not as low as what she experienced on Wednesday of the previous week. She did a lot of talking about her parts and said that she felt that "Stu" is ready to talk.*

*After the morning check-in, Doris achieved a deep trance in the guided imagery and she studied an important trauma that occurred when she was just a two-year-old. She witnessed her father rape her adolescent cousin, Jean. This story gave witness to the fact that her father could be both a good man and a monster.*

*It was obvious from her reaction that the information this story contained about her father was troubling to Doris. When he had died, she believed that he was a good man, but there were parts of her that felt differently about that. Seeing her father rape Jean gave substance to questions she had been struggling with her entire life.*

*After lunch, she shared that she had been experiencing intrusive images of this story and spent time looking at a photograph of her father. While drawing her graphic narrative, she looked confused, frustrated, and reserved. She revealed that she was having an internal battle with "Stu" over whether she could complete the story. This battle interfered so much that it was necessary to interrupt the graphic narrative and turn to a written dialogue with "Stu." They agreed that it was time to tell the story after nearly 50 years of sitting on it. She requested privacy for drawing the picture of her father raping Jean but when she tried, she lapsed into sobbing.*

*She then spent the next 45 minutes insisting that she was not capable of being the team leader and "Dot" would need to maintain that role. "I want to be Dot, but she doesn't want to be me" and "I don't cry; that is weak." She then considered what she would have to sacrifice by handing the leadership over to "Dot." It would mean being emotionally unavailable to her children and patients. Then she agreed to dialogue with her team to declare her leadership. When nobody objected, she assumed it was due to their shock and figured they were waiting her out because her history showed that she always backed down from the leadership position. She was able to resume drawing her trauma story, and it was re-presented before the session ended.*

*In the wrap-up session she reviewed the resistance by "Stu" about processing the trauma story that involved her father. She overcame the desire to throw in the towel and let "Dot" take over. She said her declaration of leadership might be surprising to her team but something that they will have to accept.*

**Day 7**

*During check-in, Doris reported that the previous night she completed a dialogue with "Stu" about his story. "Stu" felt sick and angry over the fact that he became aroused while witnessing the abuse. "Jude" then jumped into the conversation and began causing chaos. Doris informed "Jude" that tomorrow would be the day he could tell his story, and this seemed to quiet his rage. Doris said that it seemed as though "Jude" surrendered, which she attributed to the fact that all of her parts were starting to realize how much better they felt once their stories were told. A plan was made for the remainder of the week, which was to tell "Charles" and the "Bad Girls'" story, "Jude's story on Wednesday, and the death of her beloved dog Thursday.*

*In the guided imagery session, Doris examined a series of early traumatic events. The first story was an experience of being whipped with a switch by her mother, in which "Charles" was present. He went into an altered state, which consisted of his infatuation with the blood on his legs. The second story was a pre-verbal experience around two years of age, of sexual abuse by her cousin Jean, in which "Frankie" was present. The final story was at about five or six years of age, and one in which the "Bad Girls" were present. This story involved the acting out of sexual intercourse between Doris and her cousin Gail while pretending to be husband and wife. This was a rather long story and ended with Jean teaching Doris about masturbation later that night while having a sleepover.*

*After lunch, Doris was able to begin the series of graphic narratives for the stories she explored in the morning. She once again showed her leadership abilities by allowing "Charles" to work through her while drawing his story. She said that he told her what to do and compared it to "steering a car." Doris was able to talk freely about different aspects of her childhood while drawing. She discussed her belief that crying would equate to admitting defeat and that later as a mother she would never allow her children to stay with their grandparents. She could never figure out why she felt so strongly about that. While drawing the infant experience of sexual abuse by Jean, she began dissociating and had difficulty staying grounded. With assistance, she brought herself back to the present and at one point even mentioned the fact that Jean herself was most likely dissociating during these episodes of abuse.*

*Although she was unable to finish all of the drawings, Doris was off to a good start on the graphic narrative. She was able to verbalize when she felt herself dissociating and needing assistance getting grounded. Though she had more difficulty today than she had with other drawings, she was able to say that it feels good knowing that she won't be taking this big secret to her grave.*

**Day 8**

*Doris arrived at the clinic in distress and broke into tears about her guilt for not being able to forgive her father for what he did. However, she was able to pull herself together and complete the graphic narrative she had begun the day before about the sex play with Gail. She required some grounding during the re-presentation, but when it was done she said, "It's just a story now."*

*In the afternoon, she had a guided imagery session to process the trauma story in which "Jude" was "born." The story, which took place when Doris was either five or six years old, consisted of her father going into a drunken rage, shooting and killing the dog, and then raping Doris. Upon coming out of the trance state, she had no recollection of the story told during the session. The therapist had to tell the story back to her, which was the first time this information made it into her conscious awareness. She was in a state of disbelief, crying and repeatedly saying that her father told her he had killed the dog because he had mange.*

*She did not complete the entire graphic narrative but she drew the "self-repair" and "after" pictures and felt this closed things up enough for her to be able to feel safe in the hotel that night. The information in the story came as a complete shock to Doris, and she expressed that she did not know whether to be sad or angry.*

**Day 9**

*Doris reported she slept most of the night and had a good dream and no nightmares. She discovered that "Jude" was a six-year-old rather than a "hormonally charged teen on meth." He told Doris to make a list of the pros and cons about her father. She also reported being haunted by the dog's eyes. The treatment team agreed to meet with her husband on Friday. She wanted him to know everything.*

*She finished the graphic narrative and re-presentation about her pet's death. She felt it was complete and was glad that it was finally over.*

*She completed a written dialogue with "Jude" that was important in establishing a working relationship with him and validating him as an important member of Doris's team.*

*In the afternoon, she did a guided imagery about her family moving to another home when she was six. During this move, her father tricked her into playing a game and then molested her in the vehicle. After coming out of trance, Doris did not recall the details of this newly released memory, so the therapist repeated back to her what she had shared while under trance. She was not surprised to learn of her father's behavior but felt disappointed in him.*

*Doris felt she had accomplished a good amount. She felt fine to leave the clinic before drawing out the most recent trauma story. She planned to dialogue about it at night if she felt the need to. Doris reported feeling more in control of her team and confident in her ability to keep everyone safe. She felt she had found some balance with her emotions. In the past, she could not feel anger because "Jude" had sucked it up but she realized that she could be angry without expressing it in an unhealthy fashion.*

**Day 10**

*She shared a picture of her team she drew the night before and a "thank you" note to the treatment team. She also reported her daughter got her a new puppy, which Doris has named after her childhood pet.*

*She completed the graphic narrative and re-presentation of the trauma at age six. In the externalized dialogue she told the six-year-old not to worry: "It's over, use your gifts, be a six-year-old."*

*In the afternoon, the treatment team spent time with Doris's husband at her request and with her permission shared as much information as necessary. They reviewed the ITR phases, which included a discussion about the aspects of right and left-brain. They reviewed how triggers impact Doris. He asked what he could do in situations when she was so profoundly upset and he felt helpless. The*

125

*team recommended that he softly remind her that she can ground herself and state "That was then, this is now" or "You are safe with me." The team also recommended that he show respect for her need to dialogue with her parts and provide her adequate time to do so. The team did not get into details of her traumas but provided a general overview. It appeared that it was the first time he was learning about the perpetrator aspects of Doris's father. They also discussed her need for self-repair and how a new dog could provide her the comfort and healing she needed at that time. Her husband seemed a bit overwhelmed with the information but was much more receptive to the information about dissociation than Doris had anticipated.*

*The case of Doris illustrates how an intensive, marathon intervention for dissociative disorders can be done "from the bottom up," that is, starting with preverbal trauma processing rather than the presenting dissociative symptoms, which is the conventional approach. Doris's internal dissociated system was oriented toward containing and protecting the exiled traumatized parts. The unburdening of protector parts occurred from within as the exiles were liberated by bringing closure to the traumatic memories.*

*When she did the re-testing two weeks post-treatment she scored 89% on the Trauma Recovery Scale. Her other testing results were as follows:*

|  | DRS | DES | TAS | SCL | IES |
|---|---|---|---|---|---|
| Pre-Treatment | 75 | 75 | 77 | 107 | 50 |
| Post-Treatment | 05 | 12 | 66 | 30 | 24 |

## Dissociative fugue

This diagnosis is based on a person's unexpected behavior of traveling away from home with inability to remember the past. A dissociated part of the personality displaces usual consciousness and behaves differently. This would seem to be a variant of DID and an example of tertiary dissociation. Hypnosis is effective in resolving the amnesia, but the overall treatment is the same as for

DID. Usually the exploration of early traumas reveals covert alter personalities that have displaced consciousness in the past.

## Dissociative amnesia

Amnesia for early childhood or for varying periods during later life occurs frequently as a symptom in PTSD, DDNOS, and DID. It also is described as a syndrome by DSM IV-TR (American Psychiatric Association, 2000). We have seen dissociative amnesia as a symptom but so far, we have not seen one that was not a part of PTSD or the major dissociative disorders. Based on this experience, we recommend the standard trauma therapy (narrative processing and externalized dialogue) for dissociative amnesia.

## Depersonalization syndrome

Depersonalization is a state of mind that makes life seem unreal. In *depersonalization disorder* the feeling does not just come and go as it does when smoking marijuana or when a person's survival is suddenly threatened. When one's normal self seems lost and the world forever changed, that is part of a mental condition that affects millions of people worldwide. It is a misery that is poorly understood and has no generally accepted treatment. It is classified as one of the dissociative disorders.

In this condition, a person may feel numb and half paralyzed, emotionally and physically. There may be a continuous out-of-body sensation or a feeling of living in a dream or a movie. The external world may seem strange or unreal. Often individuals with depersonalization disorder have great difficulty describing their experience and they are often afraid to even think about it because it makes them feel crazy. However, they do know their experience is only a feeling and they do not actually lose contact with reality. Many people who suffered silently have found information and support from others on websites devoted to depersonalization disorder.

Many dissociative disorders and anxiety disorders (particularly panic disorder) give rise to the symptom of depersonalization. The symptom may never occur again after the person recovers from the primary disorder. When depersonalization occurs as the primary problem, it seems more difficult to treat. Psychiatric medication does not seem to be a solution. When medication helps, it does so only temporarily. The usual psychotherapy approaches have been nonspecific and long-term.

We find the causative trauma to often be extreme physical pain. When pain happens during preverbal life (from birth to age three) it may be during surgery or painful medical procedures or in unrelieved colic. It may happen by violent assault such as smothering or shaking. The infant's initial instinctual survival strategy of fight/flight by screaming and clutching fails to stop the pain. The baby lapses into the more primitive survival response, the instinctual freeze state with its near-death experience of total numbing and immobility. Although dangerous, this state does finally stop pain. The emergence from the freeze progresses through a gradual grounding in the body that reverses the void of lost spatial orientation. The transition usually involves a period of instinctual submission before the full return of bodily orientation. This phased recovery represents the instinctual response to severe pain at all ages.

In adults and children beyond age three, transitioning from the freeze state typically involves an altered state of consciousness that produces the most common symptom of depersonalization disorder—the out-of-body experience. In fact, most of the symptoms of depersonalization disorder can be understood as persisting reenactments of phases of the Instinctual Trauma Response. When the freeze state is triggered and re-experienced, the person is gripped by physical and emotional numbing. A person feels unreal and sees the world as unreal when in the throes of reenacted altered consciousness. The transitional state of automatic submission paralyzes the will and imposes a sense of automatic compliance.

When an adult's traumatic reaction to pain reaches a freeze state, the memory of the instinctual experience escapes verbal coding and is stored the same as in preverbal times. Nonverbal perceptions are like flashbulb memories, fragmented and clustered without narrative order. Lacking narrative closure, the experience seems unfinished and forever in present tense. When the trauma intrudes into current consciousness, the phases of the Instinctual Trauma Response seem like current active experience. In depersonalization disorder, the intrusions become fixed states that don't make sense in the present world.

In this light, the treatment of depersonalization disorder is straightforward. Narrative processing of the Instinctual Trauma Responses in both verbal and nonverbal realms promotes closure and conversion of the traumatic experience to past memory. Verbal narrative processing can be accomplished rapidly under hypnosis. Nonverbal processing is accomplished by the graphic narrative. The final relegation of the memory to past history is promoted by externalized dialogue with the traumatized self. The externalized dialogue may use video recording and replay or written exchange—often with automatic writing—or play therapy measures to permit dialogue by proxy.

- *Case example*

  *Fifty-year-old Martin was a therapist in a mental health center. He loved his work and felt he was at his very best until the day that he sneezed and felt a sudden pain in his head like a dagger piercing his brain. One of the arteries in his brain had ruptured. Brain surgery with clipping of the aneurysm was necessary.*

  *After surgery, he suffered transient symptoms of organic personality disorder with rage attacks and persistent memory problems. Most distressing of all, he experienced himself as a phantom hovering above and behind his body. His intelligence was unchanged. Somehow, he was able to function and even returned to his job doing psychotherapy. He constantly felt out of his body but he kept it secret and managed to struggle through for another four years before seeking help.*

  *His trauma therapy began with a hypnotic reconstruction of the surgery. He watched the operation as a Hidden Observer in the operating room. When the scene shifted to his postoperative hospital room, he visualized two Martins, side by side in the bed. The hypnotic guided imagery ended where it began in an imaginary place with Martin gazing at a loaf of bread on display in a bakery. This time there were two Martins side by side. As instructed, he stepped into the body of Martin on the left, looked at the bread, and described what he saw. Then, as instructed, he stepped into the body of Martin on the right, looked at the bread loaf,*

129

*and described it. Finally, in a climactic moment, he viewed
the bread through the eyes of both Martins at the same time
and described what he saw. The hypnotic session then
closed and he returned to the present.*

*When he re-oriented himself to the present, he smiled and
proudly announced that now he was one; he is himself again.
Satisfied with the results, he decided no further treatment was
needed. We do not know if the outcome was due to his
incomplete narrative processing of the trauma or whether he
managed to use the hypnosis itself to correct the
depersonalization. However, at the last contact six months
later, he reported that there was no return of his
depersonalization*

## Somatic Dissociation

Somatic dissociation is a term for the origin of a post-traumatic
physical symptom. These symptoms are commonly referred to as
"body memories" related to physical sensations during a traumatic
experience. It is not that the memory resides in the peripheral tissue
where the symptom is later felt, but that a dissociated memory of the
physical sensation is imprinted in the nonverbal mind. The memory is
a timeless imprint of an instant but it is experienced as timeless or
about to happen again

In treatment, verbal and nonverbal narrative processing make it
possible to identify the precise moment of the traumatic experience
when the trauma imprint was laid down. When the therapist re-
presents the graphic narrative, that precise moment can be emphasized
to promote the movement from the instant of dissociation/trauma to a
later moment thereby unfreezing the imprint. When the body memory
of that trauma state becomes integrated into the trauma narrative it
should no longer be timeless. The somatic dissociation should reverse.
We have seen this happen in cases of post-traumatic headache and
backache. However, we have also seen it fail, as illustrated in the
following vignette:

- *Case example*

  *Forty-four-year-old Arnold was paralyzed from the waist
  down due to an occupational injury that occurred 20 years
  earlier. The construction vehicle he was operating rolled*

130

*over several times and broke his back at the level of T12 with complete severing of the spinal cord. He used a wheelchair and endured extended periods of hospitalization due to complications of his injury. He developed pressure ulcers on his buttocks that required repeated surgeries. He had to catheterize himself because of a neurogenic bladder. He suffered from phantom pain in his buttocks and legs with burning sensations in his buttocks that extended down to his feet. He had paroxysmal spasms of his abdominal and leg muscles.*

*Arnold felt constantly depressed, lonely, worthless and guilty. He suffered insomnia, decreased interest in life, difficulty making decisions, and despair about the future. He had post-traumatic intrusive symptoms of recurrent images and distressing dreams of the accident. He felt detached and estranged from others. He was hypervigilant and had an exaggerated startle response. His testing results were: DES=28, TAS=82, SCL-45=140, IES=29.*

*Arnold was a good hypnotic subject and motivated in treatment, but despite all our efforts, he was not able to access the memory of the actual moment when the fracture of his spine occurred. He did access and communicate by externalized dialogue with two latent selves, the 23-year-old self from before the trauma and a pained traumatized self that blamed him for the accident, but neither of these remembered the actual moment of the fracture. We tried a variety of approaches including repeated hypnotic sessions, sand tray re-enactments, and psychodrama exploration to no avail. This was a few years before we incorporated more sophisticated parts work into our methods. In retrospect, we would search further for a latent part that held the pain of the fracture and other protector parts that kept it secret. Unfortunately, his health deteriorated and he could no longer come for therapy.*

## Pseudoseizures

Non-epileptic convulsions often occur as a reenactment of the thwarted attempt to escape being trapped in a trauma. The convulsion is usually a replay of the fight/flight survival instinct with the body straining to escape. The replay might be the imprint of an instant or of a prolonged fight/flight instinctual behavior pattern. The trauma might have been childhood sexual abuse or battering, adult rape or assault, or even traumatic surgery. The seizure might have been triggered by a stimulus outside of conscious awareness that evokes the re-experience of the traumatic instinctual state. The basic approach of sequential narrative trauma processing and parts work is effective in the treatment of pseudoseizures.

## Motor conversion symptoms

Conversion symptoms express a form of dissociative disturbance of movement or sensation (Bowman, 2006). These dissociative symptoms take the form of motor paralysis, convulsions, anesthesia, or a variety of physical symptoms. The American classification manual, DSM IV-TR, considers conversion symptoms to be different from dissociative symptoms (American Psychiatric Association, 2000). The European classification, ICD-10, considers conversion symptoms to be *dissociative disorders of movement and sensation* (World Health Organization, 1992). We believe that conversion disorder is a dissociative disorder and that the dual brain theory offers a clearer understanding of the pathogenesis.

We contend that a conversion symptom specifically relates to a latent mental system developed in the course of an Instinctual Trauma Response. We often turn to hypnosis to identify the trauma and then apply the standard trauma therapy.

- *Case example*

*The Pisa Syndrome is an abnormal leaning of a person's head or torso to one side. It is usually due to a dystonic side effect of antipsychotic medication (Suzuki, et al., 1990). Phillip, 32 years old, carried this presumptive diagnosis when he was referred for a psychiatric evaluation. He denied taking any psychiatric medication but he did have symptoms of PTSD related to a serious automobile accident two years earlier. The accident occurred on an icy hill that he was driving up when a cement-mixer truck skidded and slid downhill sideways into his car. Phillip's car was crushed and he was severely injured. As he recovered from*

132

*his broken bones and crushed tissue, he gradually developed the full triad of PTSD symptoms (intrusive, avoidant, and arousal symptoms) and also the Pisa Syndrome symptom of involuntary leaning to his right when he was startled or stressed.*

*Under hypnosis, Phillip studied his traumatic experience from the perspective of a Hidden Observer and he saw a seemingly mesmerized Phillip staring at the immense truck sliding slowly down to him. At first, uncertain about whether the truck would stop, he thought he would squeeze out of his passenger side door if necessary. The truck did not stop, but his realization was too late. His impulse to lean to the right and escape was thwarted, and he was trapped in the collision.*

*In the therapeutic narrative processing, he identified his impulse to lean to his right and escape as his thwarted intention. When it was integrated into the fight/flight experience of his Instinctual Trauma Response, it was no longer "unfinished business." It was a part of "then" rather than "now," and his Pisa Syndrome was resolved.*

## *Treatment of Medical and Surgical Trauma*

Some people who had the experience of pain and fear with medical or surgical procedures become aversive or even phobic toward doctors, clinics, or hospitals. Others may develop the PTSD triad of symptoms and some people whose medical traumas occurred during infancy may become dissociative. The helplessness of the patient during medical treatment procedures may trigger survival instincts that displace verbal consciousness and create traumatic memory. Sedatives and anesthetic drugs diminish cerebral dominance due to the greater vulnerability of the verbal language areas, allowing a nonverbal memory imprint to form the nucleus of a fear-laden traumatic memory.

Our model offers methods for both treatment and prevention of these post-traumatic conditions. The treatment methods are available for the traumatic experiences of infancy as well as of later years.

133

## Medical and surgical trauma during infancy

### Birth trauma

Birth trauma would seem to be the first possible trauma in a lifetime. However, we consider the possibility of prenatal trauma due to intrauterine tests, obstetrical manipulations, deliberate rupture of the amniotic sac, attachment of scalp electrodes, or taking scalp blood while the baby is still in the uterus. When we have a history of possible pre-birth trauma, we may add that prenatal experience to the birth trauma narrative. Possible traumatic pains during hospital delivery include: scalp wounds for electronic monitoring and blood samples, forceps extraction, being held upside down by the heels, frigid scales and utensils in a chilled delivery room, bright lights, noise, tracheal suctioning, heel lancing, vitamin injections, astringent eye medications, and irritating wiping and washing. Most traumatic of all is the abrupt separation from mother's body.

Many patients with the symptoms of complex PTSD or dissociative disorders respond positively to birth trauma processing with relief and a sense of having given words to a previously exiled part of themselves. This diminishes their trauma phobia and opens the way to full participation in the trauma processing to come. We find it helpful to show a video of a "normal" hospital delivery with its routine callous handling of the neonate to prepare the patient for the birth scene that will be studied under hypnosis or guided imagery from the perspective of the Hidden Observer.

### Neonatal ICU

Premature and critically ill newborns are subjected to many painful procedures, such as being tied or immobilized while breathing tubes, suction tubes, and feeding tubes are inserted. A study of neonates admitted to neonatal intensive care units in the Paris region of France found that large numbers of painful and stressful procedures were performed, the majority of which were not accompanied by analgesia (Carbajal, et al., 2008). Each neonate experienced an average of ten painful procedures per day. The preverbal imprints of these procedures can show up in physical symptoms and emotional reactions such as fearfulness, panic states, or depersonalization symptoms. We believe that the trait of neuroticism often follows painful neonatal experiences.

## Surgical trauma

Infants up to eighteen months of age were routinely operated upon without pain-killing anesthesia until the late 1980's (Bauchner, May, & Coates, 1992). The baby was often restrained and intubated for mechanical respiration and then given a paralyzing drug to counteract its struggle and to soften the muscles. The medical objections to infant anesthesia were that it was unnecessary because babies do not suffer pain and that the analgesic agents were dangerous. Finally, precise measurements of infant reactions to surgery proved that babies do experience pain and will tolerate anesthesia and suggested that babies had been dying of metabolic and endocrine shock following surgery without anesthesia (Anand & Hickey, 1987).

- *Survivors of infant surgery without anesthesia*

Anyone now 23 years or older who had major surgery as a baby is at risk for chronic post-traumatic illness because the surgery was probably done without anesthesia, which was the custom in most hospitals prior to 1987. Abdominal surgery for pyloric stenosis and chest surgery for congenital heart problems were the most common forms of infant surgery. Together, these surgeries were required for about eight cases per 1000 births. A rough estimate of the number of survivors during the single year 1987 in which there were 3,829,000 live births is 30,600. We do not know what proportion of these survivors are now suffering with post-traumatic symptoms, but considering the severity of the pain and the helplessness of the infant, we would expect that the majority of these infants were traumatized.

The symptom picture of the survivors we have treated is broader than the usual picture for post-traumatic stress disorder. Adult survivors report life-long symptoms of anxiety (constant nervousness and spells of terror or panic), hostility (temper outbursts and urges to smash or break things), depression, self-consciousness, distrust of others, and a vulnerability to stress. The life-long aspect of these symptoms leads to the faulty perception that they are personality traits instead of recognizing them as persisting expressions of active survival instincts first elicited by the raw pain of the scalpel. That recognition opens the way to curative treatment of the adult survivor.

135

- *Case example*

*Fifty-one-year-old Mary reported symptoms of anxiety, depression, emotional numbing, and indecisiveness as long as she could remember. She had attempted to seek healing for her symptoms through different types of psychotherapy with little success. She knew that she had major surgery as a newborn but had not considered that as a possible traumatic origin of her symptoms until she read of the little-discussed fact that before 1987 infant surgery was routinely performed without pain control. She was born with pyloric stenosis, which is an overgrowth of muscle at the juncture of the stomach and intestine. Any milk she ingested would not pass from her stomach into her intestines and emergency major surgery was necessary.*

*The kind of surgery usually done for this condition involved injecting the infant with pancuronium to paralyze the muscles. The infant would be intubated with an endotracheal tube for attachment to the respirator. No medication was given for pain. The abdominal wall would be cut open at the midline to expose the stomach and small intestine and allow excision of the lower portion of the stomach and reattachment to the upper part of the intestine.*

*Mary knew that after her surgery she was kept in the hospital after her mother went home. She was released two or three weeks later. For some weeks, she remained listless. She cried little. She had spells of limpness that gradually stopped. She also knew that there was a weak emotional attachment to her mother, who was preoccupied with a sickly older brother.*

*Since reading about infant surgery without anesthesia, she spoke to several professionals in the field of psychiatry to inquire about the impact preverbal trauma has on the brain's development but she found no leads about possible treatment until a friend told her about the treatment of her grown son at our trauma center. She immediately called and scheduled the initial telephone intake. In addition to the infant surgery, her trauma list included the failed attachment to her mother and the death of her older brother when she was four.*

136

*Mary was scheduled for a one-week intensive treatment. She accepted hypnosis to assist the guided imagery of the surgery. She was a good subject and was able to liberate a Hidden Observer part of herself to watch the surgical procedure from a safe distance. She maintained the safe distance throughout the entire surgical procedure and watched her paralyzed infant self descend into a deep freeze state, which reached a near-death episode when the surgeon incised her abdomen. She understood the ferocity of the pain and the sense that it was never ending. She had difficulty identifying the baby's self-repair but she was able to see that she did not die and that the baby was alive following the surgery. Her post-operative recovery was prolonged, and it seemed complicated by emotional numbing and hypervigilance.*

*Mary's graphic narrative fused the Hidden Observer's verbal story with the nonverbal Instinctual Trauma Response, drawing pictures labeled Before (baby being carried by nurse), Startle (infant placed on operating table), Thwarted Fight/Fight (paralyzed), Freeze (near-death state depicted as inner core of darkness), Altered State (outer darkness and timelessness), Automatic Obedience (limp submission after paralysis reversed), Self-Repair (alive though listless), and After (baby at home in her crib). Watching the re-presentation, Mary's eyes teared up in compassion for the baby but she did not relive the trauma.*

*Mary did a video dialogue with the inner baby and expressed understanding, compassion and love, which were returned by the baby. She told the treatment team that she now felt a sense of closure to the previously unfinished nonverbal memory.*

*In the days that followed, Mary did graphic narratives depicting experiences of feeling abandoned by her mother and the memory of her brother's death. She did extensive parts work, mainly dealing with her ambivalence toward her mother. At termination, she was satisfied with her therapeutic accomplishments.*

137

Adult patients not older than twenty with a history of surgery during infancy probably did receive anesthesia. Even so, the experience may have been traumatic because anesthesia—even modern anesthesia—does not necessarily prevent nonverbal awareness during surgery and post-traumatic stress symptoms do still occur.

- ### *Case example*

*A woman brought Betty, her 16-year-old daughter, to the trauma center because of failure to respond to counseling and a recent suicide attempt. She had been suffering chronic fatigue and depression with episodes of air hunger and was preoccupied with thoughts of suicide. Her history included a congenital heart disease (called "Tetralogy of Fallot") that caused difficulty in breathing and alterations of consciousness that began in the delivery room. The surgical repair done at eighteen months required opening up the heart ventricles and major arteries and reconstructing them. Betty had no conscious memory of the surgery during infancy but she was willing to process this as a foundation trauma before proceeding to other traumas.*

*The processing was done in the traditional format of weekly hour-long treatment sessions. The first session introduced her to the concept of preverbal trauma and the Instinctual Trauma Response. The second session began her generic preverbal trauma processing using the graphic narrative to depict a crib trauma with its series of nonverbal survival instinctual states. She drew herself as a baby going through the instinctual trauma phases of startle, fight/flight, freeze, and automatic obedience. She illustrated self-repair by drawing the baby reunited with her favorite stuffed dinosaur, Barney. This brought tears, which she said were not sad tears; she did not know where they were coming from. She decided to find her stuffed Barney that was still somewhere in her belongings.*

*Betty did find Barney and began keeping the stuffed toy with her constantly. Her usual crying "for no reason" did not happen while she had Barney. She brought Barney to the next session and reported that things were already different for her. She completed the drawings in that third session. In the fourth session, her pictures were pinned up in sequence on a corkboard, and the therapist re-presented the crib trauma story in both its verbal and nonverbal (instinctual states) forms. After the re-presentation, Betty completed her first externalized dialogue with her inner baby, referring to her distressed experience as "then" as opposed to "now." Betty preferred to do the dialogue on the computer rather than by video.*

*Now Betty was prepared for the processing of the known trauma, the heart surgery at eighteen months. A second therapist led Betty in hypnotic guided imagery about the surgery, including images of the intubation, incisions into the chest and heart, and the recovery room experience. The two therapists alternated sessions thereafter for the next several sessions. The processing of the heart surgery was completed in session ten.*

*She returned for seven more sessions over about four months and she and her mother felt that she had fully recovered.*

*What was important in Betty's processing of the preverbal trauma? The major trauma may not have been the surgical procedure or the fact that it was her heart that was involved. The trauma began as the baby was taken from her mother to be prepared for the surgery. The image came to Betty of the baby screaming in terror for her mother and gripping the shoulders of the nurse who carried the child down the hall. Betty thought that the inescapable feeling of terror that kept coming to her teenage self was the same feeling that she had as a baby when they took her away from her mother. She learned to console her inner dissociated baby through the externalized dialogue and to let her know that the trauma was now over.*

## Awareness during anesthesia

Because modern anesthesia consists of three agents—a painkiller, a curare-type paralyzing drug, and an amnesic agent that blocks memory of the experience—most patients do not remember awakening during surgery and therefore do not report it to their

surgeons. The curare drug prevents any struggle or gesture as sign of distress so the surgeon, the anesthesiologist, and nurse cannot see that the patient is awake. Anesthesia awakening without recall is estimated to affect between 40,000 and 140,000 patients in the United States each year (Osterman, Hopper, Heran, Keane, & Van der Kolk, 2001). Awareness with recall during general anesthesia has been reported by anesthesiologists to have an incidence of only 1.0% (Errando, et. al., 2008).

### Post-traumatic consequences

The experience of awakening in a panic during surgery and finding oneself unable to move or cry out creates a dramatic cascade of survival instincts. The drug-induced paralysis thwarts any effort to escape and deepens the instinctual freeze response. Awareness during surgery carries the exact conditions known to induce post-traumatic symptoms (Scaer, 2001). The horrors of the experience become embedded in the nonverbal mind with a potential to intrude into consciousness whenever triggered. The suffering individual will not usually relate the present-day panic to unremembered and wordless experiences during a past surgical operation.

Over half of the patients that remember becoming awake under anesthesia develop the full syndrome of PTSD (Osterman, Hopper, Heran, Keane, & Van der Kolk, 2001). Survivors with or without memory of the experience often become phobic about surgery, and their avoidance of triggers may generalize to a fear of hospitals or doctors, or of white coats. They may suffer attacks of panic or depersonalization, sometimes with clouded states of consciousness. They may repeatedly hear the voices of operating room staff. Their conditions are often misdiagnosed as panic disorder, major depression, schizophrenia, or epilepsy.

### Treatment of surgical PTSD

Once the true cause is identified, the condition can be readily treated with trauma therapy. Successful treatment requires processing of the entire traumatic experience so the therapy must be able to access that seemingly forgotten memory. The memory is there even though conscious verbal probes fail to reach it. It was not verbally coded when the person was under the effect of the anesthetics and the Instinctual Trauma Response. Even though it was stored in fragments of nonverbal perception, it can be processed into a narrative form that will be available to conscious thought and long-term memory storage.

Visualization using the Hidden Observer is effective in providing access to the traumatic memory fragments. The Hidden Observer watches the operation with a minimum of coaching by the therapist. If the patient visualizes enough details to complete a continuous narrative it will be sufficient even if some aspects are missing. The therapist can coach the Hidden Observer to closely study the paralysis and the possible body sensations. The Hidden Observer can "go inside" to detect the thoughts or feelings that the anesthetized patient has. When the narrative is drawn out in pictures and re-presented by a therapist the patient can come to own it as personal history.

- *Case example*

*In her early twenties, Anna developed a diaphragmatic hernia and began suffering deep burning pain in her chest due to regurgitation of gastric acid and digestive juices into her esophagus. When she reached fifty the pain was no longer controllable with medication, and she faced major surgery. She was apprehensive about surgery but she knew it was necessary. Her apprehension became panic when she underwent the preliminary "pH monitoring" that required a nasogastric tube inserted through her nose into her stomach. She experienced a wave of terror and felt like a helpless child. She became too afraid to undergo the surgery.*

*Her psychotherapist recognized that the terror reaction could be a flashback and her fear could be a post-traumatic phobia for surgery. The only surgery she had experienced was at age eleven when she had a tonsillectomy and she could not remember it. Her therapist referred her for hypnosis to explore the possibility that the tonsillectomy was a trauma. Anna hoped that at least the hypnosis might help her to control her fear.*

141

She was a good subject for hypnosis. She relaxed deeply and her imagery was clear and easily guided. She imagined herself admiring an item in a shop window and she was

able to follow instructions to step backwards, right out of her body, and observe herself from the outside. She accepted the explanation that she had liberated her Hidden Observer and that as the Hidden Observer she experienced an emotional detachment from Anna, which now would allow her to study Anna's surgery at age eleven, watching it as it happened right before her eyes. She could watch safely from a distance without reliving the experience.

She visualized eleven-year-old Anna with her mother in the hospital room on the morning of the surgery and she could picture the preoperative preparation, the separation from her mother, her transport on a gurney into the operating theater, placement on the operating table, draping of her head and body, and the anesthesia as it was dripped onto a nose cone. She saw Anna struggle mightily to breathe. With closer study, she identified Anna's horror that "I can't breathe and they don't know it." She could see that the child did continue to breathe and did not die. She watched the entire tonsillectomy experience and her return to consciousness in the recovery room with her mother.

With her narrative completed, Anna returned to the initial scene at the shop window and re-entered her body. Her arousal from the hypnosis was uncomplicated, and she remembered the entire narrative. The following week she returned to the clinic for the graphic narrative processing. She drew out the story in pictures that depicted each phase of the Instinctual Trauma Response and brought together the body experiences and the visual and verbal memories.

At the next visit, she did an externalized dialogue with the eleven-year-old Anna who went through the surgery. She felt that she recovered a part of herself that had been lost. She felt a sense of relief and proclaimed herself ready for the upcoming surgery—which was successful.

### Suggestions for prevention of surgical trauma

The model emphasizes nonverbal experience that occurs during a traumatic event when cerebral dominance is relinquished and the nonverbal mind is devoid of verbal guidance. Presumably, if survival instincts were not aroused, the experience under

anesthesia would not be traumatic. This suggests that a substitute verbal input that would be continuous and calming could avert the stimulation of survival instincts during anesthesia. If the anesthesiologist could be a left-brain surrogate and maintain a stream of verbal input, this should abrogate the fight/flight and freeze instincts and prevent post-traumatic complications. Perhaps this could be accomplished by continually talking to the anesthetized patient through earphones. The anesthesiologist could narrate the course of the operation in a calm and reassuring tone.

## *Treating Survivors of Orphanages*

Children adopted from orphanages in Eastern Europe, China and other countries often show the effect of trauma and institutionalization through their problems of attention, learning, and socialization. Often these children were warehoused with too few caregivers available to provide personal attention. Even when the babies were kept clean and adequately fed, they were rarely held, even during feedings. They received little visual stimulation. The walls and cribs typically were painted stark white. When adopted, the children may show problems of poor coordination and balance due to the lack of opportunities in the orphanage to crawl and explore as infants.

Their major traumas of maternal separation, neglect, and attachment failure subject them to a constant activation of their survival instincts, which can persist as lasting fixed states. Some will show prominent fight/flight states of hypervigilance and defiance while others show freeze syndromes of retarded depression or emotional numbing. The behavior of older children is disturbed by the intrusion of their younger parts representing dissociated latent mental systems from the early traumas.

Fortunately, these seemingly permanent traits are reversible by trauma therapy that provides a narrative closure to the nonverbal memories and repair for separation and attachment trauma through parts work with the inner traumatized babies.

- *Case example*

*Peter was the second Vietnamese orphan to be adopted by a suburban American couple. He was said to be nine years old when adopted, but his bone growth suggested he was actually two or three years older than that. His adoptive sister was an infant when she was adopted.*

*He fondly remembers his biological mother, who gave him up at age four or five because she could no longer feed him. She had sustained him by prolonging his nursing, but he was not getting sufficient nourishment. He was also deaf due to chronic ear infection. His mother gave him up to the orphanage so he would not starve.*

*Peter was fed in the orphanage but he was a social exile. He could not hear the staff's impatient commands. The other children bullied him. His adoption was his rescue, but the rescue he yearned for was to be with his birth mother.*

*His adoptive parents were patient and loving. He quickly entered into a close attachment to his father but he still loved his birth mother, not his adoptive mother, despite her earnest efforts. His hearing did improve with active treatment, and he was able to learn English. However, he was left with a speech impediment and he could not get over a constant dread as if he were still a fearful exile in the orphanage. He could not trust other children and, along with constant tension, he felt a constant hunger. He would gorge and still feel hungry.*

*Peter was a slow learner. He could not concentrate with a single line of thought because his thinking contained multiple streams of thought. His memory for ongoing experience was spotty, and he seemed to lose time. He suffered impulsive temper tantrums. He felt out of control most of the time and he dreaded the future.*

*It was some three years after his adoption when his sister was successfully treated for her similar problems at the trauma clinic. He saw that and he found the clinic staff to be friendly and welcoming when they saw his sister. When he agreed to his parents' suggestion that he have treatment at the clinic, he found the same warm attention he had seen his sister receive.*

*Peter was a good artist and he quickly grasped the graphic narrative trauma processing procedure. During several daylong sessions, he processed the trauma of separation from his birth mother, his starvation, and some frightening experiences in the orphanage. The ice he felt toward his adoptive mother melted, and he lost much of his hypervigilance.*

# PART 4: TRAUMA THERAPY PROGRAMS

## *Brief Intensive Outpatient Programs for PTSD and Dissociative Disorders*

We developed a program for the treatment of people from remote areas of the state where trauma therapy was unavailable and as an outpatient alternative to hospitalization for patients requiring treatment that was more intensive. The program was successful and expanded its catchment area to the United States (Gantt & Tinnin, 2007). We now treat individuals from a variety of countries around the globe.

The program treatment is based on a marathon schedule—Monday through Friday (9 AM-4:30 PM) for one or two weeks. It consists of a series of individual therapeutic procedures designed to convert traumatic memory to narrative verbal memory and to repair post-traumatic dissociation.

A multidisciplinary team administers the procedures. The patients relate to the clinic as their provider rather than to a single therapist, thereby reducing transference and dependency. The program is for outpatients only, and the patients find their own lodging. There are several hotels within a mile of the clinic. Family members accompany some patients.

### The intensive program

The initial screening is done by telephone interview after the prospective patient returns the self-administered questionnaires. If the screening shows no indication of dissociative regression, the patient is scheduled for a one-week program (in the case of uncomplicated PTSD) or a two-week program (for a dissociative disorder and/or childhood trauma).

The first day in the clinic is devoted to completing the diagnostic evaluation and an introduction to a video on the Instinctual Trauma Response. The patient also practices the treatment procedures by doing a "generic preverbal trauma processing." The patient constructs a story of an imagined experience of distress and recovery during infancy ("Imagine yourself as a young child in diapers"). He or she practices visualizing scenes from the outside during the verbal narration and when drawing the scenes. The final procedure is an externalized dialogue (Tinnin, Bills, & Gantt, 2002) with the infant self.

During the remaining days, narrative trauma processing and reversal of dissociation by externalized dialogue are applied to each trauma in turn. Normally, one trauma is processed per day in the intensive program. The day begins with morning "rounds" when the patient and staff gather to plan the day's work. The narrative processing begins with a verbal description of the traumatic experience, assisted by hypnosis if needed. The patient assumes the perspective of a Hidden Observer watching and describing the traumatic events, looking for and identifying the Instinctual Trauma Responses. The narration is video recorded.

The nonverbal narrative processing that follows is done using art therapy (Tinnin, Bills, & Gantt, 2002). The patient draws a "graphic narrative," a picture story of the trauma with special emphasis on the phases of the Instinctual Trauma Response. The graphic narrative includes at least one scene depicting each of these seven phases: the *startle,* the *thwarted intention* (to fight or flee), the *freeze,* the *altered state,* the *body sensations* (antecedents of body memories), *automatic obedience,* and *self-repair.* Each scene is drawn on a separate sheet of paper. In addition to the seven pictures listed above, the person draws "Before" and After" pictures to bracket the actual trauma. The "Before" picture sets the general scene. The "After" picture moves beyond the trauma (for example, later that night or the next day).

The therapist then tells the story of the trauma narrative to the patient with the pictures pinned to a large display board. This *re-presentation* is videotaped for later review. The combined verbal and nonverbal processing and re-telling usually achieves cognitive closure and imbues past tense to the traumatic memory. However, the final repair to accomplish is the traumatic split in consciousness that occurred in the freeze. If not repaired this could result in a lasting dissociated physiological state (Scaer, 2005, chapter 8).

The externalized dialogue is the method used to reverse dissociation. Video recording and replaying it is the preferred means to externalize a dialogue between the person in the present and the person remembered as frozen in the trauma. In the dialogue, the patient tries to recruit the old self into the present, a process that usually requires negotiation between the old and the new aspects of the person. The individual learns other forms of externalized dialogue (e.g., audio taping, writing, or using a computer to do the dialogue) that can be done at home to complete unfinished tasks. This externalized dialogue is usually the last treatment procedure of the day.

## Implications

We find that, in the absence of dissociative regression, intensive trauma therapy can proceed immediately. This is in contrast to the prevailing opinion to go slow with trauma (Foa, Keane, Friedman, & Cohen, 2009; International Society for the Study of Dissociation, 2005). We also find that with this approach the basic tasks of trauma therapy can be achieved in a relatively brief period. A time lapse between sessions is not necessary. Once patients accomplish the tasks of narrative closure and control of dissociation, they do not need time to emotionally metabolize the material. The intensive treatment is well tolerated.

## *Individual Trauma Therapy Done by a Solo Therapist*

Given that the working time for conventional individual outpatient sessions is forty-five to fifty minutes and that an initial portion of the session will have to be devoted to current events, the therapist is left with a maximum duration of thirty to forty minutes for the trauma therapy procedures. The processing of each trauma will require from six to ten sessions (one or two sessions for the verbal narrative or guided imagery; two or three sessions to draw the graphic narrative and do the re-presentation; one or two sessions for the externalized dialogue; and one or two sessions for parts work). After the second or third trauma processing, telling the verbal narrative can be combined with drawing the graphic narrative, and after the third or fourth processing the externalized dialogue time can be combined with time for parts work. The patient who has done this much processing sometimes becomes able to do

149

the drawings outside of the therapy hour. This saves time, but it still turns out that patients with extensive childhood trauma that require two weeks of the ITT marathon treatment may require at least two years of conventional weekly therapy to cover the same ground.

If the graphic processing of a trauma is unfinished toward the end of a session, there remains a double task to accomplish. First is the reminder that "that was then, this is now" and to be sure that the patient is grounded in the here-and-now. The therapist can have the patient draw the "After" picture to behold as a reminder of survival. The unfinished drawings will wait till the next session. If a re-presentation is interrupted, the therapist skips to the "After" picture and announces that this demonstrates the patient's survival. When an externalized dialogue is interrupted, the patient should assure the other participant that the dialogue will resume after this interruption, in the next session or at home.

The wisdom of processing traumas sequentially from the beginning was addressed above. The "beginning" includes the vast landscape of traumatic experience that is accumulated before the onset of verbal memory. Some of our patients found imagery of their own birth and pictured the neonatal infant startled by being projected out of the birth canal into the grip of hands, the bright light, cold air, and the chest pain of lungs filling with air, the infant screaming the protest of the fight/flight instinct, and finally the silent collapse of the freeze, before finding relief with the touch of mother's body.

Other patients have created a generic preverbal crib trauma by having the mind's eye visualize an infant in distress and allowing the scene to progress, as it will. This imaginary trauma processing is then available to the preverbal mind to bring closure to problematic adverse events outside of consciousness.

Completing the processing of a generic preverbal trauma predictably eases the patient's trauma phobia and serves as introduction to the treatment procedures.

## *Group Trauma Therapy Programs*

The primary tasks of trauma therapy can be accomplished in groups by adapting the graphic narrative and the externalized dialogue procedures to a group therapy setting. The process is more like parallel individual therapy than the usual group interaction, but the group provides another important contribution. The members become witnesses to the individual's traumatic experience and thereby promote closure to the memory, helping to transform it to a completed event.

## The process of drawing

For most groups, two therapists are required to monitor for dissociation and to provide grounding as needed. Individuals work on their own drawings with assistance from the therapists and minimal interactions with other group members. The first 60 minutes of the 90-minute group is devoted to drawing. The last half-hour is devoted to the therapist's re-presentation of completed narratives to the entire group. Usually two re-presentations can be completed. Before re-presentation and while the rest of the group members are still working, the person who finished drawing quietly tells the story to the therapist who will do the re-presentation.

## Re-presentation of the graphic narrative

The re-presentation is video-recorded for later individual review by the patient. The pictures are attached to the viewing board in sequence. The patient and the rest of the group turn their chairs to view the pictures from a comfortable distance. The presenting therapist tells the story of the pictures with some drama and empathy for the patient. The second therapist operates the camera, monitors the entire group for distress or dissociation and steps in for grounding as needed.

The re-presentation emphasizes the physiological state with each instinctual phase such as "the adrenalin rush of fight/fight," or "the shut-down of the freeze." It is often appropriate to recognize the near-death aspect of the reptilian freeze when it occurs in a warm-blooded mammal. Fixed ideas of being dead or dying in the trauma are identified. Gaps of consciousness as in a concussion are noted. Body sensations that might recur as "body memories" are pointed out and explained. Following the re-presentation, the person whose story was just told has the privilege of editing the re-presentation, adding any details that came to mind or correcting any misstatements. The therapist then invites questions and discussion by the group members.

The re-presentation in group sessions is an ideal means of providing psychoeducational material as well as promoting group cohesiveness. For example, stories about sexual abuse give the opportunity to discuss the separation of mind and body as a person enters the Instinctual Trauma Response. Group members are often surprised to find out that others have experienced unexpected and unwanted sexual stimulation, even an orgasm, during sexual abuse or assault. A particularly important issue for group discussion is usually introduced when other group members are given the chance to ask questions of the focal member: "What did your mother say when you told her?"

## Externalized dialogue for each trauma

A written externalized dialogue follows the re-presentation of a group member's graphic narrative. Written dialogues can be done by alternating hands or by different colored pen or marker.

When using alternating hands, the dominant hand writes for the voice of the present-day person and the non-dominant hand for the dissociated self or part left behind by the trauma. If the person finds too much difficulty using the non-dominant hand then using different colors will help differentiate the participants. Usually the present-day person begins the dialogue by writing an invitation to the part.

The rule for externalized dialogue is that the participants in dialogue take turns and do not interrupt. The objectives include acknowledgement of and communication with the part with the goal of unburdening the trauma-based extreme efforts. The aim is for the part to join the self in present time.

## Re-presentation of the externalized dialogue

With the person's permission, a therapist either re-presents the dialogue to the group, explaining the background and the participants and reading the text, or has the patient read it to the group. The group members can suggest further negotiation or acceptance of the solutions offered.

## Bringing closure to a session

As the time allotted for doing the drawings comes to a close, the therapists check with each member. If a person has not finished the

152

graphic narrative the group leaders urge making an "After" picture to attain partial closure to the narrative ("You can see in the "After" picture that you survived and that the trauma is over. In next week's session, you can do the other pictures to fill in the rest of the story.").

## *Trauma Therapy with Children and Adolescents*

The Adverse Childhood Experiences (ACE) Study is a major research study that looks at the correlation of current adult health status to childhood experiences decades earlier (Felitti, et. al., 1998). This study of 17,421 cases was done as a collaboration project by the Centers for Disease Control and Prevention (CDC) and Kaiser Permanente's Department of Preventive Medicine in San Diego, California. The study revealed a powerful relation between the emotional experiences of children and their adult emotional health, physical health, and the major causes of mortality.

The ACE score is derived from eight categories of adverse childhood experience: recurrent physical abuse, recurrent emotional abuse, sexual abuse, family alcohol or drug abuse, family member in prison, family member mentally ill or suicidal, battered mother, and loss of parent. The score is based on the number of categories present in a person's history. In our experience, the average child in foster placement will have an ACE score of four or more. A child with a score of four is 460% more likely to be depressed in adulthood than a child with an ACE score of zero. Foster children would be predicted to have an increased risk of attempted suicide of 1220%. One of those children would have an increased risk of later using intravenous drugs of 4600%. Without significant amelioration of their traumatic experiences, they are at high risk for the common physical diseases that shorten life (Felitti, et al., 1998). Clinicians informed of the lifelong health outcome of childhood adverse events are alert to the history of early childhood trauma in patients with chronic depression, suicide attempts, hallucinations, impaired memory of childhood, adult smoking, alcoholism, intravenous drug use, promiscuity, impaired work performance, liver disease, chronic obstructive pulmonary disease, heart disease, high rates of antipsychotic medication and anti-anxiety medication prescriptions, and elevated death rate.

Kaiser Permanente's high-volume Department of Preventive Medicine in San Diego asked over 440,000 adult individuals undergoing comprehensive medical evaluation a number of questions of newly discovered relevance, of which the following is a sample:

- *Have you ever been a combat soldier?*

- *Have you ever lived in a war zone?*

- *Have you been physically abused as a child?*

- *Have you been sexually molested as a child or adolescent?*

- *Have you ever been raped?*

- *Who in your family has been murdered?*

- *Who in your family has had a nervous breakdown?*

- *Who in your family has been a suicide?*

- *Who in your family has been alcoholic or a drug user?*

The studies of the effects of trauma on the later development of chronic diseases conducted by Kaiser Permanente and the CDC found that children who were exposed to six or more adverse childhood experiences were at double the risk of premature death compared to the lifetime of those who had not suffered these experiences. On average, the children at highest risk eventually died at age 60, compared to low-risk children who lived to age 79. Researchers followed participants through the end of 2006, using the National Death Index to discover who had died. Overall, 1,539 people died during follow-up. People with six or more ACEs died nearly 20 years earlier on average than those without ACEs (Brown, et al., 2009).

Seventy-five percent of the children and adolescents we treated had been in foster homes. Sixty percent heard voices. About one third of these young people had been treated as inpatients in psychiatric hospitals. Their average score for adverse childhood experiences as defined by the ACE Study is 4. These children bore immense burdens that would greatly increase their risk for chronic physical or mental disease and diminish their life span by twenty years (Brown, et. al., 2009) were they not treated in a program that repaired the effects of their adverse childhood experiences. These children needed to tell their stories and repair their dissociation.

## Adapting the Instinctual Trauma Response model for children

The Instinctual Trauma Response model asks that the patients tell their story and repair their dissociation. The treatment of adults with PTSD usually proceeds sequentially from preparation with education (mainly about the Instinctual Trauma Response) through narrative processing on to the repair of dissociation. The treatment of children is not as sequential. They tend to work with their dissociative parts right away—getting them onto the team—as they move into telling their story.

Children may draw the trauma story in a graphic narrative or communicate it by means of puppets, figures, or by using a dollhouse. Elementary school age children can usually be coached to use the Instinctual Trauma Response phases in their stories. Younger children can be helped to develop at least a beginning, middle, and end to a story.

- *Case example*

  *Bernard was only three years old when his adoptive parents brought him to treatment for his destructiveness. He had pulled down the curtains in his bedroom, marked all over the bedroom wall with magic markers, and had been aggressive with his adoptive mother (acting mean, bossy, and talking back). He would wake up with night terrors, screaming and kicking. He also at times would cover his eyes, cover his ears, punch himself, and bang his head on the floor. The adoptive parents had tried a variety of behavioral treatment programs, but nothing seemed to work.*

  *Bernard came to the evaluation with his two-year-old sister and his adoptive mother. He was such a little guy that no one could imagine the destruction he was able to do. His expressive language skills were poor, so he was difficult to understand. There was very little history about his birth mother and his first years of life with her. It was known that the birth mother moved around a lot and that there was severe neglect, abandonment, and physical abuse. He was taken into protective custody at the age of two.*

*Bernard was in treatment for six sessions. In each session a movie was made about Baby Bernard, using puppets, a baby doll, and other props. The first story was a generic construction depicting abandonment and neglect. The second included actual details that the adoptive mother had learned: Baby Bernard being choked, smothered, and hit with a bottle. The third was about being called names and believing them. The fourth and fifth stories were about the differences between birth mother and adoptive mother. The final story was about a known event when the birth mother threw Baby Bernard down in his crib.*

*The movies were created by the therapists using the puppets and toys and speaking for the characters during the video recording. In the first few sessions, Bernard was all over the place and seemed to ignore the story being created. However, at home he watched the video repeatedly with adoptive parents, grandparents, and his sister. He would offer information, which was then incorporated into the next video, and he became more attentive to the filming process.*

*By the sixth session, he was no longer interested in making movies. He was more interested in developmentally appropriate tasks, such as identifying colors. His adoptive mother reported that his aggressive and destructive behaviors at home had disappeared. He was quieter, more settled, and less distracted. His temper tantrums were less and more controllable through behavioral means.*

*It appeared that Bernard brought closure to his traumatic memories. He externalized his mad feelings about what happened to him in a positive way. He became able to be a normal child in a safe family.*

### Foster children as combat vets

Bo was 18 years old when he came to our clinic. He was in a pre-adoptive placement with his former guardian ad litem, who was trying to rescue him from the injustice of four futile placements in residential treatment centers from the time he was placed in the foster care system at age 8 until he left at 16. She believed that no one was addressing what was behind his severe behaviors.

He presented with a detached attitude rather like resistant combat veterans who come expecting just another treatment setting that could not help. He wished to please his pre-adoptive mother but not do anything. The staff was experienced in dealing with unmotivated individuals and asked only that he go through the motions of the treatment procedures. He intended to do nothing.

His sparse past history did include the fact that he was born prematurely and was kept in the Pediatric Intensive Care Unit (PICU) for five months. His mother was absent, and he was eventually taken home by a seventeen-year-old aunt. Our staff permitted his do-nothing stance. One therapist allowed him to lean back and listen to the story of Newborn Bo passing through the birth canal and abruptly separating from his biological mother and exiled to the PICU where he was intubated, connected to the respirator and subjected to painful procedures daily. His consciousness would cycle through awareness and animal instinct. Eventually, as his body grew stronger and his consciousness increased he was separated from the respirator and IV needles. He even discovered with one of the nurses the gaze he had missed with his mother.

One therapist started the story while a second video-recorded it. The second continued the story, using medical toys to illustrate, and Bo volunteered to do the camerawork. At some point in the interaction, Bo actually owned the story. He became animated and involved in the task with providing close-ups and dialogue for the characters. The story addressed his near-death experiences of the freeze states, his looking for his mother and the gaze, and his finding it with the nurse.

Bo was able to talk with Baby Bo (played by a therapist using a doll prop) and provided him with appropriate information about the gaze. From that point on this young domestic combat veteran helped lead the way through the rest of his treatment.

# FUTURE OF THE INSTINCTUAL TRAUMA RESPONSE MODEL

## *Advantages of Procedures in Treatment*

The treatment methods described in this book make it possible to treat both PTSD and dissociative disorders with a common set of therapeutic procedures administered in a prescribed sequence. The primary therapeutic tasks of trauma processing and resolution of dissociation bring closure to the traumatic memory and integration of the traumatized part, while the third task uses parts work to unburden dissociated parts. This treatment can be successful without an extended period of stabilization prior to trauma processing. Therapy sessions do not have to be spread out. The first two therapeutic tasks are accomplished in the sessions rather than worked through or lived out or "metabolized" between sessions. The patient begins the third task (parts work to address victim mythology) within the sessions and can independently continue to correct the misinformation of child parts using self-help measures of the internal and externalized dialogue. Full recovery can occur without the use of medication.

Complex or severely impaired individuals do not have to find gifted therapists for hope of recovery. The treatment procedures are standardized and are effective in the hands of an adequately trained therapist. Success does not depend on the personal relationship with the therapist. It does not require analysis of feelings for the therapist nor does it require a corrective emotional experience with the therapist. The procedures are adaptable to individual or group therapy and to conventional weekly sessions.

## *Research Potential*

### Manualized brief treatment for comparison studies

Our intensive program has a treatment manual prescribing each day's procedures. A participant has 30 hours of individual sessions per week for one or two weeks. Treatment outcome is measured by a panel of questionnaires, which can be administered as early as one week after termination. This time frame for treatment and outcome testing is quite practical for comparing this approach to others and for studying changes by brain imaging or physiological indicators.

A recent study by researchers at the San Francisco VA Medical Center and the University of California, San Francisco, offers a potential physiological mechanism for why people with childhood trauma tend to have a greater disease burden and more problems with aging. It might be because of their telomere biology. Telomeres are DNA-protein complexes that cap the ends of chromosomes and protect them from damage and mutations. Short telomere length is associated with an increased risk for cancer, cardiovascular disease, autoimmune and neurodegenerative diseases, as well as early death. The study collected DNA samples from 43 adults with PTSD and 47 matched participants without PTSD. The subjects with PTSD had shorter telomere length than those without. Among the subjects with PTSD, the more childhood trauma a person had experienced, the higher the risk of shorter telomere length.

A major question is whether we can have an effect on telomere biology with trauma therapy. We predict that studies of both children and adults will show that successful treatment will increase telomere length.

See a brief report of this study at:
www.ucsf.edu/news/2011/04/9776/risk-accelerated-aging-seen-ptsd-patients-childhood-trauma

# REFERENCES

Abell, A. (2000). *Talks with great composers.* New York, NY: Replica Books.

Allison, R. B. (1974). A new treatment approach for multiple personalities. *American Journal of Clinical Hypnosis, 17,* 15-32.

Alvir, J., Schooler, N., Borenstein, M., Woerner, M., & Kane, J. (1988). The reliability of a shortened version of the SCL-90. *Psychopharmacology Bulletin, 24,* 242-246.

American Psychiatric Association. (1994). *Diagnostic and statistical manual of mental disorders* (4th ed.). Washington, DC: Author.

American Psychiatric Association. (2000). *Diagnostic and statistical manual of mental disorders* (4th ed., text rev.). Washington, DC: Author.

Anand, K. J. S., & Hickey, P. R. (1987). Pain and its effects in the human neonate and fetus. *New England Journal of Medicine, 317,* 1321-1329.

Arieti, S. (1976). *Creativity: The magic synthesis.* New York, NY: Basic Books.

Bagby, R. M., Parker, J. D. A., & Taylor, G. J. (1994*).* The twenty-item Toronto Alexithymia Scale-1: Item selection and cross-validation of the factor structure*. Journal of Psychosomatic Research, 38,* 23–32.

Bauchner, H., May, E., & Coates, E. (1992). Use of analgesic agents for invasive medical procedures in pediatric and neonatal intensive care units. *Journal of Pediatrics, 121*(4), 647-649.

Bernstein, E., & Putnam, F. (1986). Development, reliability, and validity of a dissociation scale. *Journal of Nervous and Mental Disease, 174,* 727-735.

Blatt, S. J., & Wild, C. M. (1976). *Schizophrenia: A developmental analysis.* New York, NY: Academic Press.

Bogen, J. E. (1990). Partial hemispheric independence with the neocommisures intact. In C. Trevarthen (Ed.), *Brain circuits and functions of the mind* (pp. 215-230). Cambridge, England & New York, NY: Cambridge University Press.

Bowman, E. (2006). Why conversion seizures should be classified as a dissociative disorder. *Psychiatric Clinics of North America, 29*(1), 185-211.

Brown, D. W., Anda, R. F., Tiemeier, H., Felitti, V. J., Edwards, V. J., Croft, J. B., et al. (2009). Adverse childhood experiences and the risk of premature mortality. *American Journal of Preventive Medicine, 37*(5), 389-396.

Carbajal, R., Rousset, A., Danan, C., Coquery, S., Nolent, P., Cucrocq, S., et al. (2008). Epidemiology and treatment of painful procedures in neonates in intensive care units. *Journal of the American Medical Association, 300*(1), 60-70.

Coltheart, M. (1989). Implicit memory and the functional architecture of cognition. In S. Lewandowsky, J. M. Dunn, & K. Kirsner (Eds.), *Implicit memory: Theoretical issues* (pp. 285-297). Hillsdale, NJ: Lawrence Erlbaum.

Corballis, M. (1983). *Human laterality* (pp. 59-94). New York, NY: Academic Press.

Curtiss, S. (1985). The development of human cerebral laterality. In D. Benson & E. Zaidel (Eds.), *The dual brain* (pp. 97-116). New York, NY: Guilford Press.

Dell, P. F. (2009). Understanding dissociation. In P. F. Dell & J. A. O'Neil (Eds.), *Dissociation and the dissociative disorders: DSM V and beyond* (pp. 735-759). New York, NY: Routledge.

Errando, C. L., Sigl, J. C., Robles, M., Calabuig, E., Garcia, J., Arocas, F., et al. (2008). Awareness with recall during general anaesthesia: A prospective observational evaluation of 4001 patients. *British Journal of Anaesthesia, 101*(2), 178-185.

Eysenck, H. J., & Eysenck, B. G. (1975). *Manual of the Eysenck Personality Questionnaire.* London: Hodder & Stoughton.

Felitti, V. J., Anda, R. F., Nordenberg, D., Williamson, D. F., Spitz, A. M., Edwards, V., et al. (1998). The relationship of adult health status to childhood abuse and household dysfunction. *American Journal of Preventive Medicine, 14,* 245-258.

Firestone, R. W. (2001). Voice therapy: A psychotherapeutic approach to self-destructive behavior. Santa Barbara, CA: The Glendon Association.

Firestone, R. W. (1997). Suicide and the inner voice: Risk assessment, treatment, and case management. Thousand Oaks, CA: Sage.

Foa, E. B., Keane, T. M., Friedman, M. J., & Cohen, J. A. (2009). Effective treatments for PTSD: Practice guidelines from the International Society for Traumatic Stress Studies. New York, NY: Guilford Press.

Fraser, G. A. (1991). The dissociative table technique: A strategy for working with ego states in dissociative disorders and ego-state therapy. *Dissociation, 4*, 205-213.

Friedl, M. C., Draijer, N., & DeJonge, P. (2000). Prevalence of dissociative disorders in psychiatric inpatients: The impact of study characteristics. *Acta Psychiatrica Scandinavica, 102*, 423-428.

Gantt, L. (1979a). The other side of art therapy. *American Journal of Art Therapy, 19* (1), 11-18.

Gantt, L. (1979b). Art therapy. In P. Valletutti and F. Christoplos (Eds.), *Preventing physical and mental disabilities: Multi-disciplinary approaches.* Baltimore, MD: University Park Press.

Gantt, L., & Tabone, C. (1998). *The Formal Elements Art Therapy Scale: The rating manual.* Morgantown, WV: Gargoyle Press.

Gantt, L., & Tinnin, L. (2007). Intensive trauma therapy of PTSD and dissociation: An outcome study. *The Arts in Psychotherapy, 34,* 69-80.

Gantt, L., & Tinnin, L. (2009). Support for a neurobiological view of trauma with implications for art therapy. *The Arts in Psychotherapy, 36,* 148-153.

Gazzaniga, M. (2000). Cerebral specialization and interhemispheric communication: Does the corpus callosum enable the human condition? *Brain, 123,* (7), 1293–1326.

Gazzaniga, M., & Volpe, B. (1981). Split-brain studies: Implications for psychiatry. In S. Arieti (Ed.), *American Handbook of Psychiatry (2nd ed.,* Vol. 7). New York, NY: Basic Books.

Gerity, L. (1999). Creativity and the dissociative patient: Puppets, narrative and art in the treatment of survivors of childhood trauma. London: Jessica Kingsley.

Geshwind, N., & Galaburda, A. (1986). *Cerebral lateralization: Biological* mechanisms, *associations, and pathology*. Cambridge, MA: MIT Press.

Gopnik, A. (1993). Psychopsychology. *Consciousness and Cognition, 2,* 264-280.

Goulding, R. A., & Schwartz, R. C. (2002). *The mosaic mind: Empowering the tormented selves of child abuse survivors.* Oak Park, IL: Trailheads Publications.

Herman, J. (1992). *Trauma and recovery.* New York, NY: Basic Books.

Hilgard, E. (1977). Divided consciousness: Multiple controls in human thought and action. New York, NY: Wiley.

Hofer, M. A. (1970). Cardiac and respiratory function during prolonged immobility in wild rodents. *Psychosomatic Medicine, 32*(6), 633-647.

Holmes, D., & Tinnin, L. (1995). The problem of auditory hallucinations in combat PTSD. *Traumatology, 1* (2), 1-7.

Horowitz, M., Wilner, N., & Alvarez, W. (1979). Impact of Event Scale: A measure of subjective stress. *Psychosomatic Medicine, 41,* 209-218.

International Society for the Study of Dissociation (2005), [Chu, J. A., Loewenstein, R., Dell, P.F., Barach, P. M., Somer, E., Kluft, R. P., et al.] Guidelines for treating dissociative identity disorder in adults. *Journal of Trauma and Dissociation,* 6(4), 69-149

Jaynes, J. (1976). The origin of consciousness in the breakdown of the bicameral mind. Boston, MA: Houghton Mifflin.

Kernberg, O. (1976). Object relations theory and clinical psychoanalysis. New York, NY: Jason Aronson.

Kluft, R. P. (1990). Dissociation and subsequent vulnerability: A preliminary study. *Dissociation, 3*(3), 167-173.

Kluft, R. P. (1997). First-rank symptoms as a diagnostic clue to multiple personality disorder. *American Journal of Psychiatry, 155 (Festschrift supplement)*, 103-110.

MacLean, P. (1990). *The triune brain in evolution*. New York, NY: Plenum Press.

McManus, C. (2002). *Right hand, left hand.* Cambridge, MA: Harvard University.

Mahler, M., Pine, F., & Bergman, A. (1975). The psychological birth of the human infant: Symbiosis and individuation. New York, NY: Basic Books.

Mashour, G. A. (2008). Unconscious processes in psychoanalysis and anesthesiology. *International Anesthesiology Clinic, 46*(3) (Summer), 195-202.

Nijenhuis, E. R. S., Van der Hart, O., & Steele, K. (2002). The emerging psychobiology of trauma-related dissociation and dissociative disorders. In H. D'haenen, J. A. den Boer, & P. Willner (Eds.), *Biological Psychiatry* (pp. 1079-1098). New York, NY: Wiley.

Nijenhuis, E. R. S., Vanderlinden, J., & Spinhoven, P. (1998). Animal defensive reactions as a model for trauma-induced dissociative reactions. *Journal of Traumatic Stress, 11*, 243-260.

Noricks, J. (2011). *Parts psychology*. Los Angeles, CA: New University Press.

Osterman, J. E., Hopper, J., Heran, W. J., Keane, T. M., & Van der Kolk, B. A. (2001). Awareness under anesthesia and the development of posttraumatic stress disorder. *General Hospital Psychiatry, 23*, 198-204.

Parkin, A. J. (1989). The development and nature of implicit memory. In S. Lewandowsky, J. C. Dunn, & K. Kirsner (Eds.), *Implicit memory: Theoretical issues* (pp. 231-240). Hillsdale, NJ: Lawrence Erlbaum.

Perls, F. (1969). *Gestalt therapy verbatim.* Moab, UT: Real People Press.

Pinker, S. (2008). The stuff of thought: Language as a window into human nature. New York, NY: Penguin Books.

Rimland, B., & Fein, D. (1988). Special talents of autistic savants. In L. Obler & D. Fein (Eds.), *The exceptional brain* (pp. 472-492). New York, NY: Guilford Press.

Ross, C. A. (1997). Dissociative identity disorder: Diagnosis, clinical features, and treatment of multiple personality (2nd ed.). Hoboken, NJ: John Wiley & Sons.

Ross, C. A. (2000). The trauma model: A solution to the problem of comorbidity in psychiatry. Richardson, TX: Manitou Communications.

Sacks, O. (1987). The twins. In *The man who mistook his wife for a hat* (pp. 195-213). New York, NY: Harper & Row.

Salamy, A. (1978). Commissural transmission: Maturational changes in humans. *Science, 200,* 1409-11.

Scaer, R. (2001). The body bears the burden: Trauma, dissociation, and disease. Binghamton, NY: Haworth Medical Press.

Scaer, R. (2005). The trauma spectrum: Hidden wounds and human resilience. New York, NY: Norton

Schacter, D. L. (1985). Multiple forms of memory in humans and animals. In N. M. Weinberger, J. L. McGaugh, & G. Lynch (Eds.), *Memory systems of the brain* (pp. 351-379). New York, NY & London: Guilford Press.

Schiffer, F. (1998). *Of two minds.* New York, NY: The Free Press.

Schore, A. (2000). Attachment and the regulation of the right brain. *Attachment & Human Development, 2* (1), 23-47.

Schwartz, R. C. (1995). *Internal family systems therapy.* New York, NY: Guilford Press.

Siegel, D. (2010). *Mindsight.* New York, NY: Random House.

Simons, R. C. (1996). *Boo! Culture, experience, and the startle reflex.* New York, NY: Oxford University Press.

Sperry, R. W. (1985). Consciousness, personal identity, and the divided brain. In D. F. Benson & E. Zaidel (Eds.), *The dual brain: Hemispheric specialization in humans* (pp. 11-26). New York, NY: Guilford Press.

Stern, D. B. (2009). Dissociation and unformulated experience. In P. F. Dell & J. A. O'Neil (Eds.), *Dissociation and the dissociative disorders: DSM V and beyond* (pp. 653-663). New York, NY: Routledge.

Suzuki, T., Koizumi, L., Moriji, T., Sakuma, K., Hori, M., & Hori, T. (1990). Clinical characteristics of the Pisa syndrome. *Acta Psychiatrica Scandinavia, 82*(6), 454-7.

Szymanski, L. A., & Seime, R. J. (1997). A re-examination of body-image distortion: Evidence against a sensory explanation. *International Journal of Eating Disorders, 21*, 175-80.

Taylor, G. J., & Taylor, H. S. (1997). Alexithymia. In M. McCallum & W. E. Piper (Eds.), *Psychological mindedness: A contemporary understanding* (pp. 28-31). Munich: Lawrence Erlbaum.

Taylor, G., Bagby, R., Ryan, D., Parker, J., Doody, K., & Keefe, P. (1988). Criterion validity of the Toronto Alexithymia Scale. *Psychosomatic Medicine, 58*, 500-509.

Taylor, J. B. (2006). *My stroke of insight: A brain scientist's personal journey.* New York, NY: Viking.

Terr, L. (1991). Childhood traumas: An outline and overview, *American Journal of Psychiatry 148*, 10-20.

Tinnin, L. W. (1977). The Prince George's model: Applied ego psychology on the psychiatric ward. *Maryland State Medical Journal*, November.

Tinnin, L. W. (1989). The anatomy of the ego. *Psychiatry, 52*, 404-409.

Tinnin, L. W. (1990). Mental unity, altered states of consciousness, and dissociation. *Dissociation, 3*, 154-159.

Tinnin, L. W. (1994). Conscious forgetting and subconscious remembering of pain. *Journal of Clinical Ethics, 2*, 151-152.

Tinnin, L.W., Bills, L. J., & Gantt, L. (2002). Short-term treatment of simple and complex PTSD. In M. B. Williams & J. G. Sommer, Jr. (Eds.), *Simple and complex post-traumatic stress disorder: Strategies for comprehensive treatment in clinical practice* (pp. 99-118). Binghamton, NY: Haworth Press.

Tinnin, L.W., & Gantt, L. (1999). *The Instinctual Trauma Response* (videotape). Morgantown, WV: Gargoyle Press.

Tinnin, L.W., & Gantt, L. (2000). *The Trauma Recovery Institute treatment manual.* Morgantown, WV: Gargoyle Press.

Treffert, D. (2009). The savant syndrome: An extraordinary condition. A synopsis: Past, present, future. *Philosophical Transactions of the Royal Society B, Biological Sciences.* DOI: 10.1098/rstb.2008.0326.

Van der Hart, O., & Brown, P. (1992). Abreaction re-evaluated. *Dissociation, 5*(4), 127-138.

Van der Hart, O., Nijenhuis, E. R. S., & Steele, K. (2005). Dissociation: An insufficiently recognized major feature of complex posttraumatic stress disorder. *Journal of Traumatic Stress, 18,* 413-424.

Van der Hart, O., Nijenhuis, E. R. S. & Steele, K. (2006). The haunted self: Structural dissociation and the treatment of chronic traumatization. New York: W.W. Norton.

Van der Kolk, B. A. (1987). *Psychological trauma.* Washington DC: American Psychiatric Press.

Victor, B. (1983). *The riddle of autism: A psychological analysis.* Lanham, MD: Lexington Books.

Watkins, J. G., & Watkins, H. H. (1979). *Ego states: Theory and therapy.* New York, NY: W. W. Norton.

World Health Organization (1992). ICD-10. The ICD-10 classification of mental and behavioral disorders. Clinical descriptions and diagnostic guidelines. Geneva, Switzerland: Author.

Young, H. F., Bentall, R. P., Slade, P. D., & Dewey, M. E. (1986). Disposition toward hallucination, gender, and IQ scores. *Personality and Individual Differences, 7,* 247-249.

Zaidel, D. W. (1994). A view of the world from a split-brain perspective. In E. M. R. Critchley (Ed.), *The neurological boundaries of reality* (pp. 161-174). London: Farrand Press.

Zaidel, E., & Iacoboni, M. (Eds.). (2003). *The parallel brain: The cognitive neuroscience of the corpus callosum.* Cambridge, MA: MIT Press.

ᢒᢒᢒᢒᢒᢒᢒ

# Notes on Recommended Assessments

We discuss the group of assessments we have used for our trauma profile on pages 32-34. Since we developed our treatment protocol, some authors have modified and updated their scales. The citations for the original publications are in the references as well as below.

### *Dissociative Experiences Scale-II (DES-II)*

The DES-II has been revised for easier scoring. It is copyright-free and can be downloaded at: http://traumadissociation.com/des

Bernstein, E., & Putnam, F. (1986). Development, reliability, and validity of a dissociation scale. *Journal of Nervous and Mental Disease, 174,* 727-735.

Carlson, E.B. & Putnam, F.W. (1993). An update on the Dissociative Experience Scale. *Dissociation 6* (1), 16-27.

### *Toronto Alexithymia Scale (TAS)*

The *TAS*-20 is a revised and improved version of the original 26-item scale. More information on its development and psychometric properties is on http://www.gtaylorpsychiatry.org/tas.htm

A master copy of the scale, scoring instructions, reliability, validity, and normative data can be obtained for a one-time copyright fee of $40 (US) [$50 (Canada)]. Make a check payable to Dr. Graeme J. Taylor and send it to him at 130 Carlton Street, Suite 1406, Toronto, Ontario M5A 4K3, Canada.

Bagby, R.M., Taylor, G.J., Parker, J.D.A., Dickens, S. (2006). The development of the Toronto Structured Interview for Alexithymia: Item selection, factor structure, reliability and concurrent validity. *Psychotherapy and Psychosomatics, 75,* 25-39.

Bagby, R. M., Parker, J. D. A., & Taylor, G. J. (1994). The twenty-item Toronto Alexithymia Scale-1: Item selection and cross-validation of the factor structure. *Journal of Psychosomatic Research, 38,* 23–32.

### Impact of Events Scale–Revised (IES-R)

The revised version has more items so as to include arousal symptoms which were not in the original.

Weiss, D. S. (2007). The Impact of Events Scale-Revised. In J. P. Wilson & T. M. Keane (Eds.), *Assessing psychological trauma and PTSD: A practitioner's handbook* (2nd. ed., pp. 168-189). New York: Guilford Press.

Horowitz, M., Wilner, N., & Alvarez, W. (1979). Impact of Event Scale: A measure of subjective stress. *Psychosomatic Medicine, 41,* 209-218.

### Symptom Check List–45 (SCL-45)

SCL-45 (now called SA-45) is a shortened version of the original SCL-90. The questionnaire is in the public domain but the norms are not. It is now available as the "Symptom Assessment-45 Questionnaire" (SA-45) through MHS Assessments (www.mhs.com).

Alvir, J., Schooler, N., Borenstein, M., Woerner, M., & Kane, J. (1988). The reliability of a shortened version of the SCL-90. *Psychopharmacology Bulletin, 24,* 242-246.

Maruish, M. E. (2004). Symptom Assessment-45 Questionnaire (SA-45). In M. E. Maruish (Ed.), *The use of psychological testing for treatment planning and outcomes assessment: Instruments for adults* (pp. 43-78). Mahwah, NJ: Lawrence Erlbaum.

### Trauma Recovery Scale (TRS)

The TRS was developed by Eric Gentry to measure relative recovery from traumatic experiences. It can be used weekly or monthly to track response to treatment. One item on the original version is divided into two ("I feel safe" and "I am safe.") and the responses are averaged.

See pages 66-67 in the training manual on this site:

www.compassionunlimited.com/pdf/Resource/IATP CCTP
Training Manual.

Gentry, J. E. (1999). The trauma recovery scale (TRS): An
outcome measure. Poster presentation, Annual Conference of the
International Society for Traumatic Stress Studies, Miami, FL.

# DISSOCIATIVE REGRESSION SCALE (DRS)
## (Louis Tinnin, 1995)

### DIRECTIONS

This questionnaire contains six items about experiences you may have had in your daily life. To answer these items, please determine to what degree the experiences described in the questions applies to you and mark a place on the line with a vertical slash at the appropriate place, as shown in the example.

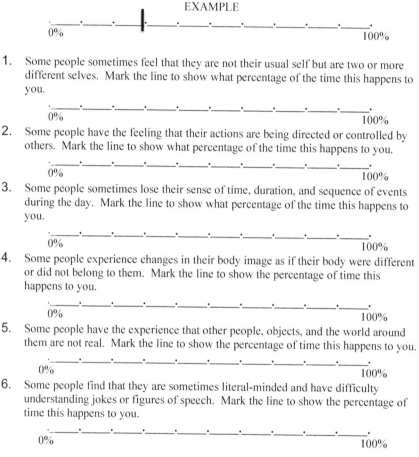

EXAMPLE

0%                              100%

1. Some people sometimes feel that they are not their usual self but are two or more different selves. Mark the line to show what percentage of the time this happens to you.

    0%                     100%

2. Some people have the feeling that their actions are being directed or controlled by others. Mark the line to show what percentage of the time this happens to you.

    0%                     100%

3. Some people sometimes lose their sense of time, duration, and sequence of events during the day. Mark the line to show what percentage of the time this happens to you.

    0%                     100%

4. Some people experience changes in their body image as if their body were different or did not belong to them. Mark the line to show the percentage of time this happens to you.

    0%                     100%

5. Some people have the experience that other people, objects, and the world around them are not real. Mark the line to show the percentage of time this happens to you.

    0%                     100%

6. Some people find that they are sometimes literal-minded and have difficulty understanding jokes or figures of speech. Mark the line to show the percentage of time this happens to you.

    0%                     100%

Note: *The DRS can be copied without charge. This assessment is used to determine whether a person has dissociative regression when used with the other assessments in the trauma profile (see pages 32-34). It has not been normed.*

# APPENDIX: Daily Report and Activity Log

## *DAILY REPORT*

*NAME* _____ *DATE* _____

1. Did you shower/bathe/wash up? _____

2. Did you brush your teeth? _____

3. Did you change into nightclothes before bed? _____

4. Did you get dressed in the morning? _____

5. Did you comb your hair? _____

6. What did you eat for:

      Breakfast? _____ Lunch? _____

      Dinner? _____ Snacks? _____

7. Did you feed/water/walk your pet? _____

8. How many cigarettes did you smoke? _____

9. Who did you talk to? _____

10. What did you buy? _____

11. What mail did you receive? _____

12. Did you take any naps? How many? _____

13. What television programs did you watch? _____

**Today I remembered _____ hours of my day.**

# DAILY ACTIVITY LOG

**NAME** _____ **DATE** _____

| **TIME** | **ACTIVITY** | **TIME** | **ACTIVITY** |
|----------|--------------|----------|--------------|
| 6:00 AM | _____ | 6:00 PM | _____ |
| 6:30 AM | _____ | 6:30 PM | _____ |
| 7:00 AM | _____ | 7:00 PM | _____ |
| 7:30 AM | _____ | 7:30 PM | _____ |
| 8:00 AM | _____ | 8:00 PM | _____ |
| 8:30 AM | _____ | 8:30 PM | _____ |
| 9:00 AM | _____ | 9:00 PM | _____ |
| 9:30 AM | _____ | 9:30 PM | _____ |
| 10:00 AM | _____ | 10:00 PM | _____ |
| 10:30 AM | _____ | 10:30 PM | _____ |
| 11:00 AM | _____ | 11:00 PM | _____ |
| 11:30 AM | _____ | 11:30 PM | _____ |
| 12:00 PM | _____ | 12:00 AM | _____ |
| 12:30 PM | _____ | 12:30 AM | _____ |
| 1:00 PM | _____ | 1:00 AM | _____ |
| 1:30 PM | _____ | 1:30 AM | _____ |
| 2:00 PM | _____ | 2:00 AM | _____ |
| 2:30 PM | _____ | 2:30 AM | _____ |
| 3:00 PM | _____ | 3:00 AM | _____ |
| 3:30 PM | _____ | 3:30 AM | _____ |
| 4:00 PM | _____ | 4:00 AM | _____ |
| 4:30 PM | _____ | 4:30 AM | _____ |
| 5:00 PM | _____ | 5:00 AM | _____ |
| 5:30 PM | _____ | 5:30 AM | _____ |

# INDEX

Printed by Amazon Italia Logistica S.r.l.
Torrazza Piemonte (TO), Italy